Contents

Published by Scholastic Ltd, Villiers House,
Clarendon Avenue, Leamington Spa,
Warwickshire CV32 5PR

Printed by Bell & Bain Ltd, Glasgow

4 5 6 7 8 9 0   9 0 1 2 3 4 5

British Library Cataloguing-in-Publication Data
A catalogue record for this book is available from the British Library.

ISBN 0-439-96537-3
978-0439-96537-8

Visit our website at
www.scholastic.co.uk

CD developed in association with
Footmark Media Ltd

Author
Lynne Broadbent

Project Editor
Wendy Tse

Editor
Sally Gray

Assistant Editor
Victoria Paley

Series Designer
Joy Monkhouse

Designer
Catherine Mason

Cover photographs
© Photodisc
© Articles of Faith
© Ingram
© Comstock

Acknowledgements

With thanks to: All Saints Parish Church, Leamington Spa; Articles of Faith; Atmosphere Ltd; BFSS National RE Centre, Brunel University; Birmingham Progressive Synagogue; Charles Farris Limited; Dale Street Methodist Church, Leamington Spa; Harrow Central Mosque; Holy Trinity Church, Leamington Spa; Islamic Relief; Lion Hudson plc; London Central Mosque; St Paul's Church, Leamington Spa; Sukkat Shalom Reform Synagogue, Wanstead.

Minimum Specifications:

PC:	Windows 98 SE or higher
Processor:	Pentium 2 (or equivalent) 400 MHz
RAM:	128 Mb
CD-ROM drive:	48x (52x preferred)

MAC:	OS 9.2 (OSX preferred)
Processor:	G3 400 MHz
RAM:	128 Mb
CD-ROM drive:	48x (52x preferred)

List of Resources on the CD-ROM

The page numbers refer to the teacher's notes provided in this book.

Home, family and belonging

Celebrations

Places of worship

Special books and stories

INTRODUCTION

This book and CD-ROM support teaching and learning in religious education for Key Stage 1 children. The legal requirement for teaching religious education in county schools is the LEA agreed syllabus, with diocesan syllabuses supporting teaching and learning in church schools. These syllabuses have common features, such as teaching about homes and families, celebrations, special places of worship and special books and stories. The non-statutory framework for religious education echoes these features in its themes of 'belonging', 'celebrations', 'symbols' and 'story'.

The CD-ROM provides a large bank of visual and aural resources around these themes. The book provides background information, ideas for discussion and activities to accompany the CD resources. All have been specifically chosen to meet the requirements for resources identified in agreed syllabuses for Years 1 and 2. Also included are photocopiable resources that enable teachers to develop and broaden these areas of study if they wish – for example, activity sheets help children to clarify their thinking or record what they find out.

The resources and activities address the two distinct attainment targets of the non-statutory framework for religious education: 'Learning about religion' and 'Learning from religion'.

'Learning about religion' engages the children in enquiry into, and investigation of religion through: the reading of religious stories; meeting people from different faith communities; visiting places of worship; and learning about festivals and celebrations.

'Learning from religion' is concerned with developing the children's capacity to reflect on their own experiences and to respond to what they have learned – for example, reflecting on the celebrations which take place in their own homes or their personal sense of belonging to a community (whether religious or secular).

Both 'Learning about religion' and 'Learning from religion' involve the development of skills, of investigation, reflection, the correct use of religious words and the recognition of similarities and differences in beliefs and practice.

Links with other subjects

Literacy
Religious education makes a significant contribution to the development of children's literacy skills. The focus on sacred books and stories provides opportunities for role-play, debate with key figures and story characters, and question time with members of faith communities.

PSHE and citizenship
In religious education, children will develop their skills of communication – they will learn to listen to others and share their own views and opinions. Children will learn about life-cycle events such as birth, marriage and death and the associated personal and community rituals. They will learn about the diverse communities within their local community, about the similarities and differences in homes, food, places of worship, special days and celebrations.

Art and design
Religion makes a rich contribution to the arts through paintings, stained glass windows, complex Islamic patterns and the symbolic design of its places of worship. Children will have opportunities to learn from encounters with the visual arts and from engaging with creative activities such as the design of cards, pictures and collages.

Music
Religions draw on a wide range of music and song in celebration and worship. Resources provide the opportunity to listen to and discuss the words of a Christmas carol and to dance to the sounds of a traditional Hebrew folk song – the 'Hava Naguila'.

History and geography
Children will learn about places of worship, old and new, in their local area. They will consult maps and plan trails. They will also learn about key religious sites and places of pilgrimage in different parts of the world. Opportunities to collect oral histories are encouraged through meeting and interviewing others in the local community.

HOW TO USE THE CD-ROM

Windows NT users

If you use Windows NT you may see the following error message: 'The procedure entry point Process32First could not be located in the dynamic link library KERNEL32.dll'. Click on **OK** and the CD will autorun with no further problems.

Setting up your computer for optimal use

On opening, the CD will alert you if changes are needed in order to operate the CD at its optimal use. There are three changes you may be advised to make:

Viewing resources at their maximum screen size

To see images at their maximum screen size, your screen display needs to be set to 800 x 600 pixels. In order to adjust your screen size you will need to **Quit** the program.

If using a PC, open the **Control Panel**. Select **Display** and then **Settings**. Adjust the **Desktop Area** to 800 x 600 pixels. Click on **OK** and then restart the program.

If using a Mac, from the **Apple** menu select **Control Panels** and then **Monitors** to adjust the screen size.

Adobe Acrobat Reader

To print high-quality versions of images and to view and print the photocopiable pages on the CD you need **Adobe Acrobat Reader** installed on your computer. If you do not have it installed already, a version is provided on the CD. To install this version **Quit** the 'Ready Resources' program.

If using a PC, right-click on the **Start** menu on your desktop and choose **Explore**. Click on the + sign to the left of the CD drive entitled 'Ready Resources' and open the folder called 'Acrobat Reader Installer'. Run the program in this folder to install **Adobe Acrobat Reader**.

If using a Mac, double-click on the 'Ready Resources' icon on the desktop and on the 'Acrobat Reader Installer' folder. Run the program contained in this folder to install **Adobe Acrobat Reader**.

PLEASE NOTE: If you do not have **Adobe Acrobat Reader** installed, you will not be able to print high-quality versions of images, or to view or print photocopiable pages (although these are provided in this book and can be photocopied).

It is recommended you use **Adobe Acrobat Reader** to zoom in to focus on specific areas.

QuickTime

In order to view the videos and listen to the audio on this CD you will need to have **QuickTime version 5** or later installed on your computer. If you do not have it installed already, or have an older version of **QuickTime**, the latest version can be downloaded at http://www.apple.com/quicktime/download/win.html. If you choose to install this version, Quit the 'Ready Resources' program.

PLEASE NOTE: If you do not have **QuickTime** installed you will be unable to view the films.

Menu screen

- Click on the **Resource Gallery** of your choice to view the resources available under that topic.
- Click on **Complete Resource Gallery** to view all the resources available on the CD.
- Click on **Photocopiable Resources (PDF format)** to view a list of the photocopiables provided in this book.
- Back: click to return to the opening screen. Click **Continue** to move to the **Menu screen**.
- Quit: click to close the menu program and progress to the **Quit screen**. If you quit from the **Quit screen** you will exit the CD. If you do not quit you will return to the **Menu screen**.

Resource Galleries

- **Help**: click **Help** to find support on accessing and using images.
- **Back to menu**: click here to return to the **Menu screen**.
- **Quit**: click here to move to the **Quit screen** – see **Quit** above.

Viewing images

Small versions of each image are shown in the Resource Gallery. Click and drag the slider on the slide bar to scroll through the images in the Resource Gallery, or click on the arrows to move the images frame by frame. Roll the pointer over an image to see the caption.

- Click on an image to view the screen-sized version of it.
- To return to the Resource Gallery click on Back to Resource Gallery.

Viewing videos

Click on the video icon of your choice in the Resource Gallery. In order to view the videos on this CD, you will need to have QuickTime installed on your computer (see 'Setting up your computer for optimal use' above).

Once at the video screen, use the buttons on the bottom of the video screen to operate the video. The slide bar can be used for a fast forward and rewind. To return to the Resource Gallery click on Back to Resource Gallery.

Listening to sound recordings

Click on the required sound icon. Use the buttons or the slide bar to hear the sound. A transcript will be displayed on the viewing screen where appropriate. To return to the Resource Gallery, click on Back to Resource Gallery.

Printing

Click on the image to view it (see 'Viewing images' above). There are two print options:

1. Print using Acrobat enables you to print a high-quality version of an image. Choosing this option means that the image will open as a read-only page in Adobe Acrobat and in order to access these files you will need to have already installed Adobe Acrobat Reader on your computer (see 'Setting up your computer for optimal use' above). To print the selected resource, select File and then Print. Once you have printed the resource minimise or close the Adobe screen using – or X in the top right-hand corner of the screen. Return to the Resource Gallery by clicking on Back to Resource Gallery.
2. Simple print enables you to print a lower quality version of the image without the need to use Adobe Acrobat Reader. Select the image and click on the Simple print option. After printing, click on Back to Resource Gallery.

Slideshow presentation

If you would like to present a number of resources without having to return to the Resource Gallery and select a new image each time, you can compile a slideshow. Click on the + tabs at the top of each image in the Resource Gallery you would like to include in your presentation (pictures, sound and video can be included). It is important that you click on the images in the order in which you would like to view them (a number will appear on each tab to confirm the order). If you would like to change the order, click on Clear slideshow and begin again. Once you have selected your images, (up to a maximum of 20) click on Play slideshow and you will be presented with the first of your selected resources. To move to the next selection in your slideshow click on Next slide, to see a previous resource click on Previous slide. You can end your slideshow presentation at any time by clicking on Resource Gallery. Your slideshow selection will remain selected until you Clear slideshow or return to the Menu screen.

Viewing on an interactive whiteboard or data projector

Resources can be viewed directly from the CD. To make viewing easier for a whole class, use a large monitor, data projector or interactive whiteboard. For group, paired or individual work, the resources can be viewed from the computer screen.

Photocopiable resources (PDF format)

To view or print a photocopiable resource page, click on the required title in the list and the page will open as a read-only page in Adobe Acrobat. In order to access these files you will need to have already installed Adobe Acrobat Reader on your computer (see 'Setting up your computer for optimal use' above). To print the selected resource select File and then Print. Once you have printed the resource minimise or close the Adobe screen using – or X in the top right-hand corner of the screen. This will take you back to the list of PDF files. To return to the Menu screen, click on Back.

HOME, FAMILY AND BELONGING

Content and skills

The theme of 'Home, family and belonging' is a common approach to teaching and learning in religious education at Key Stage 1. This approach enables children to encounter worship in the home as well as in the place of worship; the beliefs and rituals of the family and of the faith community; and the stories, special people and events which have given rise to these beliefs and rituals.

This chapter addresses the following questions: *What does it mean to belong? What does it mean to belong in Christianity? What does it mean to belong in Judaism, or in Islam? How do Christians, Jews and Muslims express their beliefs in practice?*

This chapter encourages children to think about what it means to belong to a family and to a faith community. The resources provide insight into what it means to belong within Christianity, Judaism and Islam. This reflects the breadth of study in the non-statutory national framework for religious education which states that 'Christianity and at least one other principal religion should be taught at Key Stage 1', as well as the framework's themes of belonging, believing and symbols. These are themes found in most locally agreed syllabuses for religious education, which form the legal requirement for teaching religious education.

The Resource Gallery for 'Home, family and belonging' on the CD-ROM, together with the teacher's notes and photocopiable pages in this chapter, support teaching and learning about belonging. The teacher's notes contain background information about the resources, and include ways of using them as a whole class, for group work or as individuals. Some of the activities link with other areas of the curriculum, such as literacy and art and design. Wherever possible, the activities encourage the children to ask questions and develop an enquiring approach to their learning.

Resources on the CD-ROM

The resources include images of artefacts from Christianity, Judaism and Islam that might be found in a family home. There are photographs that show how people follow their religion at home, for example, by saying grace or praying. These resources serve to develop the children's understanding of religion in the home, and what it means to belong to a faith.

Photocopiable pages

The photocopiable pages in the book are also provided in PDF format on the CD-ROM and can be printed from there. They include:

- word cards containing essential vocabulary for the unit
- an activity sheet that explores the concept of belonging
- an activity sheet on what it means to belong in a religion.

NOTES ON THE CD-ROM RESOURCES

BELONGING IN CHRISTIANITY

A Christian family home

This photograph shows the bedroom of a woman from an Orthodox Christian family. The objects on view reflect the family's beliefs and practices. Not every Christian home will have exactly the same items on display. The Bible, shown on the bedside table, is an inspiration and guide for Christians and many will read a portion of scripture each day. For Christians, the Bible is a holy book. Within the Bible, the Old Testament contains stories of Abraham, Moses and other leaders, teachings of the prophets, psalms and laws; and the New Testament recounts the life, teaching and death of Jesus as well as stories about early Christian followers.

On the shelf above the Bible is an incense holder with a cross on the top. Incense is used in Orthodox, Catholic and Anglican churches – the sweet-smelling smoke is a symbol of blessing and of people's prayers being carried up to God. The crucifix, hanging on the bedstead, is a reminder of the death of Jesus on the cross. The icons and the blessing on the wall are all associated with prayer (Orthodox Christians will pray to the saints to intercede to God on their behalf). The halos above the heads of the figures are a sign of their 'holiness'.

This photograph can be used either as an introduction to work on Christianity or to assess pupils' learning at the end of a unit on Christianity.

Discussing the photograph

- Ask the children whether they have any special objects in their bedrooms. Talk about why they are special.
- Look at the picture with the children and identify objects that they can recognise. Talk about what the objects are and why they are important.
- Prompt the children to guess what kind of a person lives in the house by observing the objects that are important to that person.

Activities

- Ask pupils to draw or paint their own bedroom or part of their bedroom, showing some of their special books, pictures or objects. Compare their bedroom scenes with this photograph.
- Ask pupils what someone could learn about their own family by looking at clues found in their house.
- Collect some or all of the objects seen in the picture of the Christian family home (such as a Bible, crucifix, incense holder, icons) for a display in the classroom .
- Invite a local Christian priest or member of the school community to bring and describe special objects which they have in their home and which reflect their beliefs .
- Look at different versions of the Bible. Read a story from one of the Bibles, for example, The Good Samaritan (Luke 10:30-37).

Picture of Jesus

Christians believe that Jesus is the Son of God. This picture shows mothers bringing their babies and young children to Jesus for him to bless them. Some of the disciples are shown watching this scene, which is based on verses in the Gospel according to Luke (18:15-17). At first, the disciples 'scold' the mothers, but Jesus encourages the children and says, 'Whoever does not accept the kingdom of God like a child will never enter it.'

Focus on the fact that children are special to Jesus.

Discussing the photograph

- Invite the children to discuss what they can see in the picture. Look at the different people in the picture; their ages; the way they are dressed; how the position of their bodies indicates their actions. Ask: *How can you tell that Jesus is welcoming the children?*
- Explain that this scene shows mothers bringing their children for Jesus to bless them.

Encourage pupils to think about what the characters might be feeling.
▶ Talk about the way the artist has tried to show the important characters by identifying them by means of a halo. Jesus and the disciples have halos above their heads.

Activities

▶ Ask the children to choose a section of the painting as the basis for their own drawing or painting – for example, the mother bringing her baby to Jesus, the two disciples, or Jesus blessing all the children.
▶ Talk about other things that Jesus did. Look at stories that Jesus told, as well as stories about the people that Jesus met and helped. For example: Jesus told parables of the Lost Sheep (Luke 15:3-7, Matthew 18:12-14) and the Lost Son (Luke 15:11-32); he healed people such as Jairus' daughter (Mark 5:21-43, Matthew 9:18-26, Luke 8:40-56) and the blind man (John 9:1-11). Jesus helped the disciples to catch fish at different times (Luke 5:1-11, John 21:2-13) and told the story of Zacchaeus (Luke 19:1-10).
▶ Look in a range of art books, Children's Bibles and pictures in stained glass to find other examples of Jesus' life and work. Notice the people who are depicted with halos and discuss why the artist wanted to show that they were special.
▶ Find, read or tell the biblical stories that link with the images of Jesus' life and work. Encourage the children to retell the stories through their own artwork or through role-play.

Mary and Child

This painting focuses on the mother and child image of Mary and Jesus. This image is frequently seen in churches, on icons, in paintings and on Christmas greetings cards. The artist has not tried to portray a real mother and child but to convey a religious truth – that Jesus, the baby, God's Son, would grow to be the man who would die on the cross; hence the 'baby' in the picture is not actually a baby but a small adult.

The painting of an icon is a great skill and the artist will select the materials with care and in a spirit of prayer. The making of an icon is thought to be an act of worship in itself. Icons are used by Christians, usually in the Orthodox tradition, as a focus for their prayers and worship. On entering an Orthodox church, individuals will often stand before one of the icons and pray before the communal worship begins.

Discussing the photograph

▶ The power and beauty of the icon would best be viewed on a large scale. Allow the children to study the image in silence before talking about it.
▶ Ask the children what images they can see on the icon. Who are the people painted on it? Are there clues that indicate their identity? For example, the halos shown above the heads indicate their importance. They may notice the figures on either side of the central scene, but focus on the painting of Mary and Child.
▶ Ask the children how the characters relate to each other. For example, the mother's head is turned towards her son, while the son is pointing towards his mother.
▶ Talk about the artistic features of the picture, the colours used by the artist and the feelings that the picture evokes in the children. Does it evoke feelings of awe because of the rich colours, of calmness because of the expressions on the mother and child's faces, of happiness, or even of sadness.
▶ Discuss places and times when the children might have seen images like this one before, perhaps in churches or on greetings cards or posters.

Activities

▶ Make a collection of mother and child images for display. Family photographs, pictures from newspapers and magazines as well as postcards and greetings cards could all be used as part of a collage. Compare the icon images with the photographs and pictures collected, noting the similarities and differences.
▶ Invite the children to make their own mother and child painting or drawing, either based on the icon image or on one of the other photographs or pictures on display. Having spoken about the seriousness with which the icon painter chooses the materials, encourage the children to do the same. Take time to note the posture of the mother and child, and the relationship between the two.

▶ If possible, visit an Orthodox church in the area to look at the icons inside and to learn how they are used for prayer. If there is no Orthodox church in the local area, a Roman Catholic priest or parent might be able to speak to the children about images of Mary and the child Jesus in their own church or home.
▶ Mary and the child Jesus are often the subject of hymns and songs, particularly those sung at Christmas. Help the children to learn some suitable songs, such as 'The Virgin Mary had a Baby Boy' and 'Little Donkey'. Encourage them to think about the words and compare them with the visual images.
▶ Use visual images to create a display on the theme of 'Mother and Child'. Use the display, together with the hymns and songs to form part of an assembly or service for the festival of Christmas.

A selection of crosses

This picture shows different examples of crosses: two rosaries, a plain wooden cross, and a palm cross. The cross is an important symbol in Christianity. It is a reminder or symbol of the death of Jesus on the cross – an event that is marked by Christians in services on Good Friday. A cross with the image of Jesus on it is called a crucifix. Most crucifixes show a suffering Jesus, but some, such as Epstein's 'Christ in Majesty' in Llandaff Cathedral, Cardiff, show Jesus in triumph with his arms outstretched. For Christians, this is a joyful symbol. An empty cross (like the third cross in the picture) is a symbol of the risen Christ and is therefore a Christian symbol of hope. A cross is usually found outside and inside almost all churches and indeed traditional churches are built in the shape of a cross. Many Christians will make the sign of the cross with the words 'In the name of the Father, and of the Son and of the Holy Spirit', when praying as a symbol of their faith.

The first two crosses in the picture are part of rosaries. Rosaries are used by Christians, mainly by Roman Catholics, for prayer. Whilst the person is praying, they move the beads through their hands, stopping at each bead to recite either the 'Our Father' (the 'Lord's Prayer') or a 'Hail Mary'.

The palm cross is distributed in churches on Palm Sunday as a reminder of Jesus' entry into Jerusalem when people threw palm fronds on the ground before him as a sign of welcome.

Discussing the photograph

▶ Ask the children what similarities and differences they can see in the crosses in the pictures. Explain what the crosses are and what they symbolise.
▶ Discuss with the children whether, and where, they have seen crosses like those shown in the picture. Some might have noticed a cross outside a local church or might themselves have a cross and chain.

Activities

▶ Make a collection or display of crosses using this picture along with the ones of 'Three crosses' and 'Crucifix' (see below). Other places to find crosses include text books, on copies of the Bible, or crosses on chains.

▶ Invite the children to create their own plain crosses. Draw, paint or model crosses in clay. Think about why the cross is special to Christians, identify key words such as *Jesus* and *hope*, and add these to the design.
▶ Visit a local church and 'hunt the crosses' to be found there. If the church is built in a traditional shape, walk around the outside to look at the different aspects of the cross-shape. The cross may also be seen on gravestones.
▶ Invite a priest or minister to speak to the children, explaining why the cross is important and to show them how to make

the sign of the cross. Suggest that they explain how, and why, the sign of the cross is made when baptising a baby – to show that the baby has now joined God's family.

▶ Walk around the local area and spot symbols of the cross on religious bookshops, on greetings cards (such as Easter, baptism and confirmation cards), in jewellery shops and on war memorials.

Three crosses, Crucifix

These three crosses tell the story of Easter. The palm cross is a reminder of Jesus riding on a donkey, entering into Jerusalem as a hero, the week before he died. The people welcomed him, shouting 'Hosanna' and tearing down palm leaves or fronds to throw at his feet. Palm trees are common trees in the Middle East, and there would have been many palm trees in and around Jerusalem. The palm tree can be regarded as a tree of life, for it provides dates to eat, leaves under which to shelter from the hot sun, fibres for ropes and baskets and fuel for fires. Today on Palm Sunday, Christians remember this event and churches give out palm crosses and hold processions around the church or local area.

The crucifix is a reminder of Jesus being crucified on the cross, an event which Christians remember on Good Friday with services in church which tell about all the events leading to Jesus' death. People also eat hot cross buns on this day.

The empty cross is a symbol of hope because Christians believe that Jesus rose from the dead, and they celebrate this on Easter Day. Chocolate Easter eggs, the eggs being a symbol of new life, are eaten on this day. Orthodox Christians usually make hard-boiled eggs dyed with vegetable dye on Easter Day to symbolise new life. (See chapter 2 'Celebrations' for more information about Easter.)

Discussing the photograph

▶ Discuss the similarities and differences between the three crosses, for example the similarities of shape, differences of materials and style.

▶ Use the three crosses to tell the children about the Easter story. Talk about what each of the crosses symbolises.

▶ Discuss the image of Jesus on the crucifix. Discuss the children's responses to that image. Explain how the image reminds Christians about part of the story of Jesus. It is a sad image for Christians. However, it is not the end of the story and the empty cross is a symbol of hope.

Activities

▶ Tell the story of Jesus arriving in Jerusalem on a donkey and the crowd welcoming him as a hero. Encourage the children to think about how the crowd would feel. What might they have said or shouted out to welcome Jesus.

▶ Role-play the story of Jesus' return to Jerusalem, using palm fronds the children can make out of sugar paper.

▶ Use these pictures with the resources for Easter in Chapter 2 'Celebrations' to create a display on Jesus and Easter. Use the three crosses as the central symbols to hold a class discussion about Palm Sunday.

▶ Make Good Friday and Easter Sunday displays. The Good Friday display should be set out on a purple cloth – the traditional colour used in churches at this time. It should include objects and symbols to remind children of the Good Friday story. Ideas include an open Bible, a crown of thorns, a dice (the Roman soldiers threw dice for Jesus' robe), a crucifix, a tomb made from papier mâché, hot cross buns.

The Easter Sunday display should be set out on a white or gold cloth and should include objects and symbols to remind the children of the Easter Day story such as an open Bible, a tomb made from papier mâché (but this time with the stone rolled away), an empty cross, coloured hard boiled eggs/chocolate Easter Eggs, flowers.

▶ Using the objects and symbols as prompts, and a Children's Bible, tell the Good Friday and Easter Day stories. Ask the children to retell the stories using the prompts to help them.

▶ Use instruments to compose 'sad' and 'joyful' music to accompany the retellings of the Good Friday and Easter Day stories.

▶ Look at the words of a selection of Easter hymns and songs and discuss the 'feelings' that they represent.

▶ Visit a church during the period of Lent which precedes Easter to look at the Easter

Garden. Also look at any pictures or stained glass windows that depict the crucifixion and resurrection. Ask the priest or minister how Easter is celebrated in their church.

Statue of St Francis

This is a statue of St Francis, shown with two doves; his left hand is raised in blessing. St Francis is often known as St Francis of Assisi, the town in Italy where he was born in 1181 or 1182 - the exact date is unknown. Francis was the son of a rich man and when he was young, he was a soldier and fought in battle. One day he was praying at the church of San Damiano near Assisi, and he heard a voice saying, 'Francis, go and repair my church which is falling into ruin'. Francis believed it was the voice of God and from that time, he gave up his money and rich clothes and went to live with the poor, teaching them about God and helping the sick.

It was Francis who first arranged a nativity scene with 'Mary' and 'Joseph' and real animals to help people understand about the birth of Jesus. Francis loved all of God's creatures and there is a story about how he calmed a savage wolf by speaking to the wolf and asking the village people to feed the animal so it did not have to kill to find food. Francis wrote the Canticle (song) of Brother Sun, praising God's creation. One of the verses says, 'Be praised my Lord, for Brother Wind and for the air, and for the clouds, the clear sky and all kinds of weather by which you nourish all your creatures'.

The statue of St Francis is wearing the brown robes of the Order of Franciscans, which is an order of monks founded to follow his teachings. The knots on the rope around his waist stand for the promises the Franciscans make when they join the order. One of these promises is the promise of poverty: that is, not spending your life seeking wealth.

Saints are regarded as very special Christians who have tried to do God's work. The saints are often mentioned in prayers and some Christians, especially Roman Catholics, might pray to the saints and ask them to intercede on their behalf to God – they believe that saints are so special that they have the power to ask God to help other people. The children should know that not all Christians believe this, and many Christians think that you can speak to God directly.

Discussing the photograph

- Show the picture of the statue to the children and ask them what they notice about the figure of St Francis.
- Tell the children about St Francis and that he started an order of monks. The monks all follow his teachings.
- Talk about the doves. This is a way of showing that St Francis loved all animals and believed that all were God's creatures. It might be appropriate to talk about the dove as a symbol of peace and to recall the story of how Noah sent a dove out of the ark to see if there was any dry land (the dove returned with an olive branch in its mouth).
- Ask the children whether they have heard of any other saints; it might be that there are local church schools named after saints. Talk to the children about who saints are.

Activities

- Read or listen to stories told about St Francis of Assisi. Role-play some of the episodes in his life, for example, setting up a nativity scene to explain the story of the birth of Jesus to the villagers; or re-enacting the story of the savage wolf.
- Look at a version of 'The Canticle of Brother Sun'. Each verse contains the words, 'Praise to you, my Lord for...' and refers in turn to Brother Sun, Sister Moon and Stars, Brother Wind, Sister Water, Brother Fire and Sister Earth. With the children, collect words to describe each of these aspects of creation and encourage them to write their own 'canticle' or song, either individually or in groups, using the format of the original version for guidance.
- Learn about the stories of some other saints, beginning with those whose names are given to local schools. Gain information from school brochures, from a visit by the headteacher or through exchanges with the pupils (either in person or through e-mail contact).

Saying grace

This is a picture of a Christian family saying grace together before the family meal. Grace is a short prayer said to thank God for the food that will be served during the meal. It is often a time for remembering those who do not have enough to eat. 'Graces' usually begin with the words, 'Thank you God for...' and may refer to the food that is to be eaten, the people who have grown or made the food, such as the farmers, the bakers, and those who have prepared it for the table. One example of a traditional 'grace' is: 'For what we are about to receive, may the Lord make us truly thankful'. It is not only Christians who say grace before eating, Jews also do this and the practice may be found in other religious homes.

Discussing the photograph

▶ Show the picture to the children and ask them what they think the family might be doing. There are clues in the picture as some of the family members have their eyes shut and their heads bowed and the family have clearly not started to eat the food on the table.

▶ Discuss the reasons why the family might be saying a prayer to God at this time, making links between saying a prayer and receiving food.

▶ Introduce the idea that grace often refers to people who do not have enough to eat. Discuss the reasons why some people do not have enough food.

▶ Talk about times when people have thanksgiving celebrations, such as the Christian harvest festival, or the Jewish festival of Sukkot.

Activities

▶ Collect some examples of prayers said before meals. These might be examples from the children or examples found in prayer books or text books. Invite the children to write their own grace. (Be aware that writing a 'grace', which is essentially a prayer, may be inappropriate for some or all of the children.)

▶ Conduct a thanksgiving exercise as a circle time activity. Brainstorm all the things that the children are 'thankful' for. This includes their homes, their families and pets.

▶ List and illustrate the things that the children are thankful for in a class book. Share the book with other classes or during assembly.

BELONGING IN JUDAISM

A Jewish family home

This picture shows the interior of a Jewish family home, the objects on view reflecting the family's beliefs and practices. The capel, sometimes called a kippah, a small 'skull cap', is shown on the back of the chair. It is worn by men and boys during prayers and when the holy book, the Torah, is studied. Some orthodox Jewish men and boys wear the capel all the time and in progressive synagogues, some women, in particular women rabbis, may wear a capel. It serves as a constant reminder of God's presence – as though God's presence is over you.

The Seder plate, seen on the bookshelf, is used on the first night or the first two nights of Passover (Pesach), a festival celebrated during the spring. It is a time when Jews remember the story of how God, through Moses, led the Jewish people out of slavery in Egypt under the Pharaoh, to a new life of freedom. On the Seder plate there are foods that remind the family of the period when their ancestors were slaves and which help them to retell that story during the family Seder meal which is shared at the beginning of Passover. (For more information about the Seder meal and Passover, see Chapter 2, 'Celebrations'.)

The nine-branched candlestick, the hanukiah, with a box of Hanukkah candles, is also shown on the bookshelf. The hanukiah and candles are used at Hanukkah, a festival lasting eight days and celebrated in November or December (depending on the lunar calendar), which commemorates the freedom of the Jewish people to live and worship in their own chosen manner.

The picture on the top left of the bookshelf depicts the Western Wall in Jerusalem, which is sometimes refered to as the Wailing Wall. The wall is all that remains of the temple that was used during biblical times and is now a special place for Jews and Jewish identity. Praying at the Western wall has been a Jewish custom for centuries and often Jews will place written prayers in its cracks.

The picture can be used either as an introduction to work on Judaism or as a task to assess pupils' learning at the end of a unit on Judaism.

Discussing the photograph

▶ Invite the children to talk about the special things they have in their homes and bedrooms. They should think about the reasons why they are special, when they play with or use the objects, and what they feel about these things.

▶ Show the picture to the children and ask them to identify objects which they recognise. Encourage them to use their knowledge to guess what kind of a person lives in the house from observing the objects which are important to them.

▶ Focus on the Seder plate and the hanukiah; the plate is a symbol of the special meal which the family shares together at the beginning of Passover and the hanukiah is used during a festival when special candles are lit. Discuss with pupils the times when they might have special meals with their families or times when candles are lit.

Activities

▶ Using paper plates, ask each child to illustrate their favourite or special meal. Share these illustrated favourite or special meals with the rest of the children, talking about when and where they have their special meal, and who they would share this with.

▶ Make links between the children's special meals and the Seder meal, shared in a Jewish family or in a Jewish community. Talk about how the Seder meal is a time for remembering a special story.

▶ Make a display of candles which are lit at special times.

▶ Ask the children to identify different places in the world which are special to their families, such as countries of origin or the homes of relatives. Make displays of these. Make links between the special nature of these places and the special significance of the Western Wall for Jewish families.

▶ Use this picture with 'A Christian family home' and 'An Islamic family home' to start a display 'Home and family' or 'Why my home is special'. Encourage the children to bring in or draw pictures of their homes and rooms that are special to them.

Mezuzah on front door, Mezuzot and scroll

'Mezuzah' is a Hebrew word meaning 'doorpost'. The mezuzah is the parchment scroll that bears the words of the Shema (found in the Torah), as seen in 'Mezuzot and scroll'. Both pictures show examples of different mezuzah cases.

Scripture in the book of Deuteronomy in the Torah states that Jews should love God with all their heart and with all their soul, and that God's words should be in their hearts, taught to children, talked about in the family, and written on the doorposts of the family home. In order to remember these teachings and to fulfil this commandment, this text is written on a scroll, sealed in the mezuzah case and nailed to the front door of a Jewish home. It is nailed to the right hand side of the doorpost, about a third of the way from the top and slightly pointing inwards. Mezuzot (plural) are also attached to the doors inside the house, but not on the bathroom.

The scroll is handwritten by a specially trained scribe, and the script is therefore liable to smudging should water permeate the mezuzah case. The mezuzah case has to be inspected regularly to ensure that this has not happened because any smudging may alter the meaning of the Hebrew words and the scroll is not then 'kosher', meaning fit for religious use. The mezuzah would then have to be replaced.

The mezuzah symbolises the inner beliefs of the Jewish family. When they enter their home, members of the family touch the mezuzah with their fingers, or kiss their fingertips, as a constant reminder of God's words. Mezuzah cases may be made of different metals, or even pottery, and with different designs. However, many designs will include the Hebrew letter 'shin' – the first letter of the first word written in the parchment scroll, 'Shema' meaning 'hear'. This letter is clear on the mezuzah cases in 'Mezuzot and scroll'.

Discussing the photographs

▶ Show both pictures to the children and introduce the mezuzah as a further symbol of a Jewish family home, which is nailed to the outside front door post.

▶ Ask the children to look closely at the picture of 'Mezuzot and scroll' – in particular at the cases. Ask them to spot the similarities and differences between the four mezuzot.

▶ Explain that the mezuzah is a special piece of holy text from the scriptures. This text tells

Jews to love God with all their heart and soul, and that God's words should be in their hearts, taught to children, talked about in the family, and written on the doorposts of the family home. This is why it is nailed by the front door.

▶ Explain that the mezuzah or the scroll is written in Hebrew, and the first letter of the text is commonly seen on the mezuzah cases. Ask the children to find the Hebrew letter 'shin' both on the mezuzah cases and on the scroll – it is shaped rather like a 'w'.

▶ Tell the children that Hebrew is read from right to left and that there are no letters for vowels; vowels are represented by dots and dashes written in particular positions. It is therefore a difficult language to read.

▶ Talk about the opening words that are written on the mezuzah scroll: 'Hear, O Israel, the Lord is our God, the Lord is One'. The word 'Hear' is a command to all Jewish people, and the name 'Israel' in this context means 'all Jewish people'.

▶ Discuss what it means to a Jewish family to have a mezuzah case with its scroll nailed to the front of their homes and what visitors to the home can discover about the family from the mezuzah.

Activities

▶ Make a mezuzah case from card or from clay. For a card mezuzah case use a net made from a small box (such as a raisin box). Decorate the mezuzah case with Hebrew writing and symbols such as the Hebrew letter 'shin' and the Star of David.

▶ Make a mezuzah scroll by using paper soaked in a weak solution of tea to create authentic-looking parchment. Write the opening words of the Shema in black ink on the 'parchment'. Roll the scroll and insert it into the children's own mezuzah cases.

▶ Use the class collection of mezuzahs to create a brightly-coloured display. Encourage the children to use ICT skills to reproduce the opening words of the Shema in large lettering for the display.

▶ Visit a synagogue or, if possible, a Jewish shop to see the mezuzah in situ.

▶ The mezuzah is an outward sign of a family's religion and it's something that all visitors will see upon entering the house. With the children, talk about how visitors could learn about a family if they did not see something as visible as a mezuzah on the front door. Use other resources provided on the CD, such as 'A Christian family home' or 'An Islamic family home', to talk about other signs that tell us about the family who lives in that home.

Star of David

The Star of David is properly named the Magen David (Hebrew), or Shield of David. It is a six-pointed star which is said to represent two interlocking 'd's', the first and last letters of the name of David, who was the first king of Israel in biblical times. It is a fairly modern symbol in Judaism and is shown on the flag of Israel. It can also be seen on the outside and inside of many synagogues and, in this picture, it is shown as a necklace on a chain.

Discussing the photograph

▶ Ask the children to look carefully at the Star of David on the necklace. Can they see the shapes of the two 'd's' which make up the star?

▶ Discuss how the symbol is a reminder of King David, the first king of Israel.

▶ Talk with the children about other symbols which may be worn as necklaces.

Activities

▶ Visit a synagogue to search for the Star of David symbol both inside and outside the building.

▶ Invite a Jewish visitor to school to talk about and show examples of the Star of David on jewellery or on other objects in their home, especially those brought from Jerusalem.

▶ Find the Star of David on an Israeli flag (available on the internet). Compare this with other symbols on flags, for

example, the dragon on the Welsh flag or the Maple leaf on the Canadian flag. Discuss the importance of these symbols and make some flags to display in the classroom.

Lighting the hanukiah, Hanukiah and dreidels

Hanukkah is a festival lasting eight days. As Judaism follows the lunar calendar, the date of the festival changes from year to year, but it usually occurs during November or December.

Hanukkah is a time to remember when the Jews were persecuted by the Syrian Greeks. The Greek King Antiochus who ruled the country did not allow the Jews to worship God in their own way. He made the Jews bow down to the Greek idols; placed idols in the temple, the holiest place for Jews; and desecrated the temple by requiring the sacrifice of pigs (a non-kosher animal) on the altar.

The Jews decided to rebel and formed a small army led by Mattathias the Hasmonean and his son Judah the Maccabee. Although small in comparison to the mighty force of the Syrian Greeks, the rebel army defeated the opposition.

When the Jews cleansed the temple of the idols and tried to light the temple lights to show that the place was fit for the worship of God, they discovered that there was only enough oil for one day, and it would take eight days to obtain more oil for the temple lights. However, a great miracle happened and the oil lasted for eight days until more oil could be brought. This is the significance of the hanukiah, the special menorah (candelabra) that is used during Hanukkah. The hanukiah consists of eight candles in a row, plus a central ninth candle, the shammash or servant light, which is used to light the other candles. On the hanukiah in the photographs, the ninth candle is the one in the middle which is raised higher than the others. The candles on the hanukiah are lit in a particular order. On the first night of Hanukkah, the servant candle is lit and the first candle is lit. The candles are allowed to burn down, which usually takes about 25 minutes. On the second night of Hanukkah, a new servant candle is lit and two candles are lit from the servant light, and so on throughout the eight days of the festival. The candles are placed in the candle holders from right to left and are lit from left to right, so the photograph 'Lighting the hanukiah' shows the candles being lit on the fifth night of the festival.

The photograph 'Hanukiah and dreidels' shows the candles on the final day of Hanukkah. Traditionally, the hanukiah is placed in a window to advertise the Jews' freedom. Work by the light of the hanukiah is not permitted, so an alternative is to play games. A popular game is the dreidel, using a spinning top with a Hebrew letter on each of its four sides. Many children play the dreidel game during Hanukkah. It is a game for between four and six players and is played with coins, nuts, wrapped sweets or counters. At the start of the game each player puts a coin or sweet into the 'pot'. The dreidel is then spun and whichever Hebrew letter lands face up, the player must act accordingly. The letters are shown as follows:

Examples of plastic dreidels are shown in the picture, but a dreidel can be made from a square of card marked with four letters, with a matchstick in the centre.

Discussing the photographs

▶ Before discussing these pictures, sit quietly with the children for one minute in a darkened room. Light a candle and ask the children to sit quietly for another minute. Ask the children to describe their feelings when they were in darkness, and then when the candle was lit.

▶ Show the children the two pictures and explain that they show a special candle that is used during the Jewish festival of Hanukkah in winter.

▶ Using 'Lighting the hanukiah', explain the festival of Hanukkah and why the number of candles is significant. Count the number of candles with the children.
▶ Look at the brightly lit candles in 'Hanukiah and dreidels'. Ask the children to imagine the feelings of the family when the candles on their hanukiah are all lit.
▶ Tell the children that many Jewish children like to play games by the light of the hanukiah. Look at the dreidels in the picture and explain the dreidel game to them.
▶ Ask the children to identify times when the lighting of candles has special meanings, for example, birthday candles to show the age of a person, Advent Candles or a Christingle signifies the light of God coming into the world in the form of Jesus at Christmas.

Activities

▶ Borrow a hanukiah or make a class hanukiah. The eight lights in a row can be made from a series of eight thumb pots fashioned in modelling clay, with a ninth thumb pot, higher than the rest in the middle. This will be the servant light. Hanukkah candles can be purchased from resource centres or from most synagogues around the time of the festival.
▶ Tell the story of Hanukkah in a simplified form. Encourage the children to role-play the story or retell it using puppets.
▶ Light the hanukiah on each of eight days after learning about and retelling the story. It is forbidden to work by the light of the hanukiah, so encourage the children to think of fun ways to spend their time. Make some dreidels and play the dreidel game.
▶ It is traditional to eat foods cooked with oil during Hanukkah to remember the story about the miracle of the oil. Supervise the children to make some potato latkes (potato and onion cakes fried in oil) with supervision, or buy some frozen latkes and heat them in a microwave. Doughnuts are also eaten at this time.
▶ Visit a synagogue during Hanukkah, or invite a member of the community to school to teach the children some songs traditionally sung at Hanukkah.

SHABBAT

Celebrating Shabbat

This picture shows how Jews welcome Shabbat, the Sabbath into their homes. The candles, challah loaves and wine are used at Shabbat, the Sabbath – the Jewish festival that is celebrated every week. Shabbat begins at sunset on Friday evening and lasts until sunset on Saturday evening. It is a festival which recalls God's creation of the world and his rest on the seventh day.

Before sunset on Friday night, the mother will light two candles to mark the start of Shabbat. Before the evening meal, the father will say a blessing over the kiddush cup, (shown in the picture next to the bottle of wine) thanking God for the fruit of the vine, and a blessing over the two loaves of challah to say thank you to God for the fruits of the earth. After each blessing everyone shares firstly the wine, and then the sweet challah bread. The white challah cover is placed over the bread before it is blessed. (For more information about Shabbat see below.)

Discussing the photograph

▶ Ask the children to look at and identify the objects shown in the picture.
▶ Focus on the two candles. Tell the children that at least two candles are lit as a sign that this is the start of a special day, Shabbat. Discuss occasions when they light candles on special days, such as birthdays or festivals.
▶ Focus on the wine and the bread and discuss how these are made. The wine is made from red grapes and the bread from wheat – things that grow from the land.

Activities

▶ Recreate the Shabbat meal by collecting some or all of the objects seen in the picture. You do not need special candlesticks but could use any two 'silver' candlesticks with white candles. If a kiddush cup is not available, a small stainless steel goblet or a small 'cut glass' wine glass might be used. Instead of wine, use red grape juice.
▶ Make challah loaves or rolls. A recipe can be found in Leah W Leonard's book *Jewish*

Cookery (Crown). The loaves or rolls are usually plaited.

- Make a cover for the challah using a rectangle of white cloth decorated with coloured pens. The decorations, as those on the challah cover in the picture, should show that this is a special cover used at Shabbat. For example, the decorations could include two candlesticks, the two loaves, flowers and Hebrew writing if a stencil with Hebrew writing is available.
- Use this picture with the audio resources for the Shabbat blessings (provided on the CD – see below) for an extended discussion on Shabbat.
- Learn a Shabbat greeting – 'Shabbat Shalom', which means 'A peaceful Sabbath!'

Audio: Shabbat blessing, Audio: Blessing over the wine, Audio: Blessing over the bread, Lighting the Shabbat candles, Blessing over the bread at Shabbat

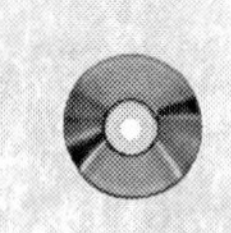

Before Shabbat begins the home will be cleaned and the family will prepare for the Shabbat meal on Friday evening and for all the other meals to be eaten during Shabbat. Shabbat is a day of rest so once Shabbat begins, no work can be done – that is no cleaning, no shopping, and no homework. Also, on Shabbat, no flame can be lit as this would be an act of creation on a day of rest, so families may have an urn to ensure hot water for hot drinks and time switches for lights and for the cooker, to provide cooked meals. Shabbat is a time for the family to go to the synagogue, to visit friends and to relax together.

Just before sunset, the mother will light two candles. The photograph 'Lighting the Shabbat candles' shows the mother motioning her hands over the flames to bring the light and holiness of Shabbat in. She then says the blessing in Hebrew, translated as 'Blessed are You O Lord our God, King of the Universe, who commands us to light the Sabbath lights'.

Before the evening meal, the father will raise the kiddush cup of wine and say the blessing in Hebrew, translated as 'Blessed are You O Lord our God, King of the Universe, who creates the fruit of the vine.' Everyone tastes some of the sweet wine – children may have grape juice. Then there is a blessing over the bread: 'Blessed are You O Lord our God, King of the Universe, who brings forth bread from the earth.'

The photograph 'Blessing over the bread at Shabbat' shows the father cutting the bread, and everyone will then taste a small piece of the bread. The children of the family are then blessed – a parent, usually the father, places his hands on their head and says a blessing (see 'Blessing the children at Shabbat' below). The family then sit down and enjoy a Shabbat meal together. The lighting of the candles, the blessings and the tasting of the wine and the bread mark the start of this special day, a weekly day of joy, when the family remembers God's creation of the world.

Discussing the audio clips and photographs

- Before listening to these audio resources, tell the children that they will be listening to blessings that are said over the objects shown in the picture, 'Celebrating Shabbat' – to mark the start of the special day of the week, Shabbat.
- Talk to the children about why Shabbat is celebrated in the Jewish faith. Use the photographs to illustrate what is done before and during the first Shabbat meal on the Friday night.
- Discuss with the children the words spoken in the blessings over the wine and the bread and make links between thanking God for the 'fruits of the earth', and Shabbat as a day when Jews remember God creating the world.
- Discuss the idea that Jews, Christians and Muslims all believe that God created the world. Some believe that He created the world in six days and then rested on the seventh day, exactly as it says in scripture, others believe that God created the world but that 'six days' is not a precise measure, it simply means that it took some time.

Activities

▶ Compare this resource with 'Saying grace' (see above) and talk about the similarities between the Hebrew blessings said over the wine and the bread, and the grace said before eating in the Christian family.
▶ Set a table for Shabbat using these audio resources and the photograph 'Celebrating Shabbat' (see above) as a guide. You will need: a white tablecloth, two candlesticks with white candles, red grape juice, two challah loaves with a cloth to cover them, place settings, cutlery and plates, serviettes.
▶ Bring in the food and drink at Shabbat for the children to taste: sweet challah, which can be purchased from a supermarket or made by the children, and red grape juice.
▶ Make a zigzag (concertina) book to show how Shabbat is celebrated by a Jewish family. Use key words to label the drawings such as: two candles; plaited challah; red wine or grape juice; blessings.
▶ Focus on the blessings said over the wine and challah bread, all thanking God for the 'fruits of the earth'. Brainstorm those things for which the children are thankful; these may include food and drink but also people who are important. Make drawings or a collage of these things to be remembered for an assembly or a classroom display.
▶ Read or tell the story of creation from the book of Genesis in the Bible. Use a Children's Bible or a storybook retelling, or see the Story of creation in Chapter 4 'Special books and stories'.
▶ Visit a synagogue to meet a Jewish family or invite a Jewish mother or father to school to describe how they prepare for and celebrate Shabbat in their home.

Blessing the children

The picture shows a Jewish father blessing his children on the Friday evening of Shabbat. He is blessing them by putting his hands on their heads and reciting a prayer which includes the words: 'May God bless you and guide you. Be strong for the truth, charitable in your words, just and loving in your deeds'. He concludes with the priestly blessing: 'The Lord bless you and keep you; the Lord cause his face to shine upon you, and be gracious unto you; the Lord lift up his countenance towards you and give you peace. Amen'.

Shabbat is welcomed into the home and God is thanked for the love, happiness and security which the family brings. Blessing members of the family (in some homes the mother is blessed as well as the children) is a way of dedicating the family to God. The image of a traditional family ritual and a happy family home might be difficult for many children who cannot share in this experience, but the feelings expressed in the picture can be explored in a wider context.

Discussing the photograph

▶ Ask the children to talk about what might be happening in the picture. Have any of the children seen someone putting their hand on another's head, as in this picture? Some children might have seen this take place in church, or have seen images of the Pope doing this. Discuss what the action might mean.
▶ Introduce the idea of saying a blessing in words and actions. Discuss the meaning of the simple form of blessing, 'May the Lord bless you and keep you'.
▶ Talk about the blessing that is given to the children at the beginning of Shabbat and what it means.
▶ Ask the children to identify words to describe how the father and the children might be feeling. Do they appear happy or sad? How might the father be feeling towards his children at this time?
▶ Ask the children to look for clues in the picture that show them when this scene is happening. They should notice the Shabbat candles, the wine and the challah bread.

Activities

▶ Focus on the blessing and its meanings – a blessing asks for good things such as care and protection to be given to the person who is blessed. For whom would the children like to ask for good things? Make a collage of names or pictures of those people who are special to the children.
▶ Talk about the good things that the children would like to ask for, for the special people in their lives. Blessings are very different from 'gifts' – they are to do with values; those things

which cannot be seen but which are important to us throughout life.

- Develop a class or group 'blessing' or 'wish list' with words and phrases from the children. This should be done as a secular rather than a religious activity as it would be inappropriate to begin with the words, 'May the Lord bless...' in a classroom, and with children who are not from a faith tradition.
- Use all the resources about Shabbat provided on the CD, and ask groups of children to provide a commentary about what happens in a Jewish home at Shabbat.
- Ask the children to imagine that they are a Jewish boy or girl and that they are inviting a friend for the Friday evening meal. Use the picture resources about Shabbat that are provided on the CD to describe to the friend what they will see on that evening.

Audio: Jewish music (Hava Nagila)

This is an extract from the 'Hava Nagila' hora, a Hebrew folk song. The title means 'Let us rejoice'. The 'hora' is a traditional Israeli dance – it is usually danced at joyous occasions such as weddings or Bar Mitzvahs. Its inclusion here is to provide a 'flavour' of Israeli culture rather than any specific links with the religious festivals above. It does, however, provide an opportunity for children to learn a traditional Israeli song and dance.

Discussing the music

- Tell the children that this is a piece from a traditional song from Israel, and it is traditionally accompanied by Hebrew words. It may be helpful to indicate where Israel is on a map of the world.
- Discuss with the children how they feel when they listen to the music. Is it sad or happy? Is it music to listen to when you are sitting still, or moving about?
- Discuss the instruments which might make the sounds heard.

Activities

- Learn to dance the hora. The basic movements are simple and can be varied according to the age and abilities of the children:
    1. The children form a circle, holding hands.
    2. The children move five steps to the left. This can be done stepping with the left foot and moving the right foot next to the left, or, passing the right foot behind the left.
    3. The children move five steps to the right. This can be done stepping with the right foot and moving the left foot next to the right, or, passing the left foot behind the right.
    4. The children take three steps forward into the circle and joyfully throw their hands, still joined, into the air.
    5. The children take three steps back, back into the larger circle and repeat from step 2.
- Learn the first few words of Hava Nagila:

Hava Nagila, hava Nagila, hava Nagila,
V'nis m'cha ('ver-nis m-cha', with the 'ch' pronounced as in 'loch')

- Sing and dance Hava Nagila during an assembly or during a multicultural day in school.

BELONGING IN ISLAM

An Islamic family home

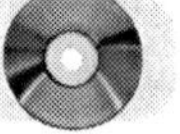

The picture shows the interior of a Muslim family home, the objects reflecting Muslim beliefs and practices. On the table is a copy of the Qur'an, the holy book, written in Arabic and believed by Muslims to be the words of Allah, God. On the left wall, there is a picture displaying the 99 names of Allah and this links with the prayer beads on the table. There are 99 beads and a Muslim will remember the 99 names as he or she moves the beads through their fingers. The topi, or cap, on the table is worn by some men, though not all, for prayer. Beside the table, on the left, is a prayer mat, which is used for prayer at home or in locations other than the mosque. The prayer mat is placed on the floor facing towards Makkah, and in particular towards the Ka'bah, which is shown in the picture on the right-hand wall. The Ka'bah is the cube-shaped building in the centre of the grand mosque in Makkah. There are also two pictures of Arabic script on the table, and the inclusion of the plant is no accident – the natural world is a symbol of Allah's creation.

The picture could be used either as an introduction to work on Islam or as a task to assess pupils' learning at the end of a unit on Islam.

Discussing the photograph

▶ Before looking at the picture, ask the children to think about the objects they have in their sitting rooms or bedrooms, which of these objects are of particular importance to them and the reasons why. The objects might not be of any monetary value but may remind them and their family of special events or people.

▶ Ask the children to identify objects that they recognise in the picture and use their knowledge to guess what kind of person lives in the house from the objects which are important to them.

▶ Discuss the use of the individual objects and the links between some of them – for example, the picture depicting the 99 names of Allah and the 99 prayer beads.

Activities

▶ Highlight and discuss in turn the individual objects in the picture. Ask the children, in pairs, to talk about each object, using the word cards on photocopiable page 30 to help them.

▶ Learn the correct words for each of the objects: Qur'an, Ka'bah, tasbir (or prayer beads), prayer mat, topi (or cap). Encourage the children to write their own word cards or captions to label the picture.

▶ Play 'I spy': one child has to describe an object without telling everyone else what the object is. The rest of the children guess and name the object.

▶ Make a display of some or all of these artefacts in the classroom.

Reading the Qur'an at home

This picture shows the family reading the Qur'an together at home. For Muslims, the Qur'an is the word of Allah, revealed to the Prophet Muhammad. The Qur'an is written in Arabic and, from a very young age, children attend the mosque school after their day at school, to learn to read and then recite the Qur'an. The boys in the picture have their heads covered with topis and the girls are wearing hijab as a mark of respect when reading the Qur'an. Islam teaches that modesty in dress is important for men and women. Reading the Qur'an is a form of worship.

Discussing the photograph

▶ Before introducing the picture, talk about the children's special books and why these books are special. Perhaps they were their first baby books, presents from relatives or the first book they learned to read for themselves.

▶ Talk about the times when they have read or looked at books together with their parents and relatives.

▶ Discuss with the children who they can see in the picture. Talk about how the people are dressed – in particular, the fact that everyone has their head covered.

▶ Focus on the book or books that are being read by the family. While the father and the older children appear to have copies of the Qur'an, the younger children appear to have shorter texts.

▶ Talk about the links between the covered heads and the reading of the Qur'an. Muslims traditionally cover their heads when praying. The photo depicts how the covered heads are a sign of the importance of the Qur'an for the family, and a sign of respect.

Activities

▶ Make a display of the children's special books and stories, with captions as to why these are favourite books and stories.

▶ Look closely at a copy of the Qur'an, noticing the Arabic writing and the decorative borders around the pages.

▶ Invite a Muslim to speak to the children about why the Qur'an is so special to Muslims.

▶ Read or tell a story from the Qur'an using a suitable storybook for children. The Qur'an includes many stories that the children may already be familiar with, such as the stories of Jonah and the Whale, Abraham and the Holy House, and Joseph and his amazing dreams.

The Ka'bah at Makkah

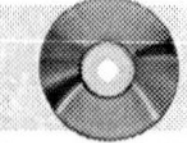

The picture shows the Ka'bah, a cube-shaped building in the centre of the Great Mosque in Makkah, Saudi Arabia. Makkah is said to be the birthplace of Muhammad, and the Ka'bah is the holiest place in Islam. The Ka'bah became the first house for worshipping the One True God, Allah, at the time of the Prophet Muhammad, although the Ka'bah itself is said to have been built by Adam and rebuilt by Ibrahim. The Ka'bah is covered with a huge cloth, richly embroidered with Arabic writing. This cloth or 'kiswa' is replaced each year. During daily prayer, Muslims throughout the world place their prayer mats facing towards Makkah and the Ka'bah for prayer. Every Muslim will try to make a pilgrimage to Makkah once in their lifetime. The picture shows the pilgrimage, or hajj, when Muslims circumambulate the Ka'bah. Behind the arches of the grand mosque two minarets (tower-like structures) can been seen. It is from these minarets that the call to prayer is given by the muezzin five times a day.

Discussing the photograph

- Ask the children whether they can recognise anything in the picture. They may have seen the Ka'bah and the minarets on prayer mats.
- Focus on the Ka'bah: talk about its shape and its size in relation to the people; notice the beautifully decorated cloth which covers it.
- Focus on the people: point out that most of the people are wearing white. The ihram is the two pieces of cloth worn during the pilgrimage that symbolises that everyone is equal before God. Do the children notice that the people are moving in the same direction around the Ka'bah?
- Tell the children that Makkah is the holiest place in Islam and that all Muslims will try to go there once in their lifetime. Encourage the children to look for clues which suggest that Makkah is a thriving city with a large population.

Activities

- Make a drawing or a model of the Ka'bah using a cube-shaped box. Decorate the drawing/model to show the cloth placed over the Ka'bah.
- Send a postcard from Makkah. Tell the children to imagine that they are standing near the Ka'bah and are sending a postcard to a friend. They should draw the picture and describe what they can see.
- Look at a map showing the UK and Arabia. Look at the distance between the two places and discuss how a Muslim from the UK would make the pilgrimage to Makkah.
- Invite a local travel agent to describe how the journey to Makkah could be made.
- Invite a Muslim who has made a hajj to Makkah to describe how they prepared for the journey and the events which happened when they were there. If this is not possible, use a suitable video on the hajj.

PRAYER IN ISLAM

Prayer at home

The picture shows prayer or 'salah' in the family home. The man and the women have their heads covered for prayer and each person has his or her own prayer mat. The prayer mats are slightly different from each other, but each mat provides a clean space for prayer. Before beginning to pray, each person will have performed wudu – the ritual washing of the hands, the arms, the face and the feet. The prayer mats and people are facing towards Makkah, with the man and boy in the front and the women in a row behind. In the mosque, women may pray behind the men or in a separate room (for both cultural reasons and reasons of modesty – the prayer positions include forward prostration on the prayer mat

and it is thought immodest for a man to be placed behind a woman.)

In Islam, Muslims are required to pray five times a day: before sunrise, at noon, in the afternoon, at sunset and at night. Prayer, or Salah, for Muslims is one of the Five Pillars, (or five obligations) for every Muslim. Daily prayers can be made anywhere – at home, at the place of work, as well as at a mosque. Most Muslims will try to visit the mosque for noon prayers on a Friday. Visitors to Muslim countries may see Muslims performing Salah in the open air. A clean place is required for prayer and this is the reason that Muslims will ensure that they have access to a prayer mat.

Discussing the photograph

▶ Discuss with the children how our actions can have special meanings. For example, waving your hand to mean 'hello' or 'goodbye'; putting up a hand to show that you know the answer to a question. Lead them to consider actions that people make when praying. In the Christian faith, people make the sign of the cross and may join their hands in prayer.

▶ Display an enlarged copy of the picture and reveal each person at a time to focus attention on the individuals and their positions. Identify words to describe the posture of each person. For example, the woman on the extreme left is kneeling back on her heels with her hands on her knees.

▶ Talk about the whole family. Look at how they are all facing in the same direction, and how everyone except the young boy has their head covered.

▶ Focus on the man and boy and the girl in the middle of the row of women. Ask the children to think about what the position of the hands might show.

▶ Tell the children that the Arabic word for prayer is Salah.

Activities

▶ Play a game, 'Actions speak louder than words', to help the children 'read' the picture resource. Identify actions which have meanings. In pairs or as a whole class, one child mimes an action, and the other children have to guess the meaning. Include a familiar action for prayer, such as putting hands together and closing eyes.

▶ Look at a range of picture books which show people 'in action' and ask the children to describe the action and its meanings.

▶ Encourage the children to think of as many words as they can to describe the positions of the people in the picture. Ask the children why they chose certain words. Use these words to develop a word bank or to create labels and captions for the picture.

▶ Invite a Muslim to show the prayer positions or alternatively watch a video clip of a Muslim family praying.

▶ Compare this picture with other resources on the CD, such as 'Saying grace' and audio clips of the blessings for the Shabbat meal. Talk about how people can pray or worship at home in a variety of different ways.

Performing wudu

In this picture the boy is performing 'wudu', the ritual washing before prayer. This boy is using a bowl of water but could also use running water from a handbasin or the bath. In the mosque, there are usually separate washing rooms for men and women. The purpose of wudu is to ensure physical cleanliness before prayer but it is also symbolic of spiritual cleanliness and readiness for prayer. A Muslim begins his wudu by saying, 'In the Name of Allah' and then washes his or her hands up to the wrists, three times. The mouth and nose are rinsed and then the face is washed. The arms are then washed to the elbow and water

rubbed over the ears and head. Finally, the feet are washed up to the ankles. Following this ritual washing, the person has fully prepared him or herself for prayer.

Discussing the photograph

- Before looking at the resource, ask the children how often they wash their hands during a day.
- Discuss the reasons why the children wash their hands during the day, such as after going to the toilet, after playing football, before meals, before going out or before going somewhere special.
- With the children, identify words and phrases which describe how they feel after washing or having a bath, for example: clean, fresh, no dirt.
- Describe what is happening in the picture. Encourage the children to describe how the boy looks.
- Introduce the idea that the boy is preparing to pray which is a special time for him.
- Tell the children that this ritual is not just an ordinary wash – it is called 'wudu' and it represents spiritual cleanliness before prayer.

Activities

- Make a chart of the times and frequency of the children's hand washing.
- Write with the children a 'step by step' approach to washing hands.
- Using the resource, talk about the different times of the day the boy, Amir, washes his hands to prepare for prayer. Explain how Amir will pray five times a day (before sunrise, at noon, in the afternoon, at sunset and at night) and will therefore perform wudu before prayer at these times.

Prayer mat, Compass

The prayer mat provides a clean and comfortable space for prayer. Prayer mats may be made from a number of different materials, the ones in the picture being like a woven carpet. Others may be made from a lighter nylon material which makes it easier for a Muslim to carry when travelling. The designs and colours of prayer mats vary, but often a mosque and minarets are depicted, as in the prayer mat in the picture. The edges of the mat depict geometric patterns while other mats include leaf or flower designs. Figures are never depicted on prayers mats, nor are they shown in mosques. Everything about the design of a Muslim's prayer mat seeks to focus the mind on Allah alone. Prayer mats are placed facing towards the Ka'bah in Makkah and this prayer mat incorporates a compass, with the position of Makkah indicated for the user.

Beside the prayer mat is a small cap or topi which is often but not always worn by men during prayer times. Also pictured are prayer beads, with the 99 beads symbolising the 99 Names for Allah.

Discussing the photograph

- Talk about the different shapes of the buildings seen on the prayer mat – the domed mosque, the tall minaret behind it, the four pillars in the foreground, the arch shapes of the mosque.
- Talk about the different patterns that can be seen – the geometric shapes on the border and on the floor tiles of the mosque.
- Look at the close-up picture of the compass on the prayer mat and talk about what a compass is used for in general. Ask the children to explain why there is a compass on the prayer mat.

Activities

- Design a class or small group prayer mat using a large sheet of paper or piece of material. Invite some of the groups to make geometric or flower and leaf designs on the design of the mat. Let other children contribute the dome or minaret shapes. Display the children's prayer mat/s in the direction of Makkah.
- Use a map and a compass to find the direction of Makkah in relation to the UK. A compass specifically designed for Muslims to use would be helpful.
- Look at the photographs 'Prayer mat', 'Compass', 'Performing wudu' and 'Islamic prayers

at home'. Ask different groups of children to explain how Muslims prepare for prayer and the manner in which they pray.

▶ Make a zigzag (concertina) book on prayer in Islam.

Prayer beads and cap

The picture shows a simple, crocheted cap or topi; it is often, but not always, worn by men for worship. There are also two sets of prayer beads or tasbir. The larger set of prayer beads contains 99 beads, each bead standing for one of the 99 names for Allah. Muslims will pass the beads through their fingers, remembering one of the names for Allah with each bead. The smaller set of prayer beads contains 33 beads and these would be passed through the fingers three times to complete the 99 names.

Discussing the photograph

▶ Ask the children to describe what they can see in the picture and whether they have seen any of the artefacts before.

▶ With the children, count the number of beads on each set. Ask them if they can think of a connection between the two sets of prayer beads, one with 33 and the other with 99 beads.

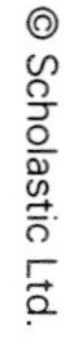

▶ Talk about the fact that Muslims have 99 names for Allah to describe all the different aspects, such as, guide, friend and creator.

▶ In order to talk about the cap, use this picture with 'Islamic prayers at home' and 'Reading the Qur'an at home'. Discuss who might wear this cap and when it might be worn. Encourage the children to think about the cap being worn as a mark of respect when worshipping. Compare the wearing of the capel, small skull cap, by Jewish men in worship.

Activities

▶ Encourage the children to think of different ways to describe themselves. Emphasise that they are not just one thing, but there are many different 'sides' to a person. Ask the children to draw a picture of themselves and to think of five words to describe themselves. For example, son/daughter, brother/sister, cousin, friend, pupil, Brownie/Cub Scout. Ask the children to add another five words to describe their personality or qualities. For example: kind, friendly, happy, helpful. Are these enough words to provide a good description of themselves?

▶ Make links between the number of names needed to describe a person and the 99 names which Muslims have to describe Allah. Refer back to the picture of 'An Islamic family home' to look at the picture of the 99 names written in Arabic on the wall of the family home. Ask the children to imagine what some of these names might be.

▶ Choose some of the 99 names and ask the children to copy these out for display in Arabic or English.

▶ Discuss the meaning of the names. Ask the children to think of a symbol to illustrate them. Some examples would be a map for 'the Guide', or plants and animals for 'the Creator'. Explain that, at no point should the children try to draw Allah, as this would be inappropriate in Islam.

▶ Make a display of the names, illustrations, the beads and a print out of this picture of the prayer beads and cap.

Video: The Call to Prayer at home

The Call to prayer, or 'the Adhan', is given five times a day before the time of prayer. The Call is as follows:

Allah is the greatest (x4)
I bear witness that there is no god but Allah (x2)
I bear witness that Muhammad is the Messenger of Allah (x2)
Hurry to prayer (x2)
Hurry to success (x2)
Allah is the greatest (x2)
There is no god but Allah

This Call is usually given from the minaret, the tower next to the mosque, by the muezzin (the man who gives the Call). This video clip shows a father giving the Call to Prayer in the family home, followed by a recitation of the prayers. Prayer mats are set out and the family take their places for prayer. Prayer in Islam involves a set pattern of positions, of standing, bowing and prostrations while reciting the prayers. Each set of positions is called a rak'ah.

Discussing the video

- Watch the video and explain that this is an example of Islamic prayer.
- Tell the children that some people pray in silence while others recite prayers. Ask them to sit in silence for two minutes to experience this absence of sound.
- Ask the children to sit in silence and listen to the Call to Prayer. Explain that the Call is given in Arabic and that the actions are as important as the words. They are all part of the act of praying because they show that the worshipper submits to Allah.
- Talk about the feelings of the children as they listen to the Call. Is the sound happy, sad, or exciting?
- Discuss other methods of calling people to prayer. For example, church bells that are rung before a service.
- Look at the text of the Call to Prayer and discuss what the Call says about Allah and about Muhammad.

Activities

- Discuss and list with the children the sounds that they like to hear, and the sounds which call them to do something. For example, the alarm clock to wake them up.
- Talk with the children about the sounds they hear each day, and discuss with the children what it would be like to live in a world without sounds.
- Make a chart of the times of day when the Call to Prayer is given. (The BBC website provides a prayer calculator www.bbc.co.uk/religion/religions/islam/index.shtml). Look at the times on the chart and ask the children to think about what they are doing at these times.

Phases of the moon

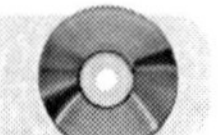

The Muslim calendar is divided into twelve months but these are lunar months, with 29 or 30 days in each month. The moon and its phases are therefore very important in Islam. This is especially true of the month of Ramadan, the time when Muslims go without food and water during the hours of daylight. (See Chapter 2 'Celebrations' for more information about Ramadan.) The moon was also an important guide for those travelling in the desert and the crescent moon with a star in its crescent is a well-known symbol for Islam.

Discussing the picture

- Encourage the children to describe what the moon looks like during these phases.
- Identify the terms used to describe the moon in particular phases: crescent moon, half moon, full moon, waxing and waning moons.
- Introduce the children to the idea that some cultures divide the months of the year according to the cycle of the moon (they have lunar months). The word 'month' comes from the word 'moon'.
- Talk about the times when the children might be able to spot the moon while they are doing this unit of work.

Activities

- Using photocopiable page 57 'Following the moon' (Chapter 2 'Celebrations'), ask the children to fill in the times when they spot the moon during one month and to draw the shape of the moon as it changes over the month. If possible, do this task during the month of Ramadan – the month when Muslims fast from sunrise to sunset.
- Invite a Muslim to speak to the children about the importance of the moon to Muslims; as a symbol for Islam; as a means of calculating the months; and as a way of knowing the start and end of the month of fasting, 'Ramadan'.
- Draw the symbol of Islam, the crescent moon with the star in the crescent. Display the symbols around the classroom, along with symbols from other religions.

Video: What prayer in Islam is like

The video shows two Muslim girls discussing how they prepare for prayer and how they feel when they pray. The girls state that their parents taught them how to pray when they were very young. They say that they wash before prayer in order to be clean before praying to Allah. The washing, apart from being a physical cleansing, is also symbolic of preparing oneself spiritually for prayer to Allah. Praying to Allah makes the girls feel closer to Allah and it reminds them to 'do good things'; that is follow the teaching of Allah, throughout the day.

Discussing the video

- Listen and watch the video, and then ask the children what this tells them about Islam.
- Talk to the children about why they think people pray. For example, to thank God for something good; to ask for help.
- Discuss with the children where and how people pray.
- Discuss with the children why washing before prayer might help the Muslim girls.

Activities

- Collect and display pictures of people praying, showing many different positions for prayer.
- Invite a visitor, from any faith tradition to talk with the children about how he or she prays in their faith community.
- Look at some examples of prayers from Christianity, Judaism or Islam and talk about their meaning.

NOTES ON THE PHOTOCOPIABLE PAGES

Word cards

PAGES 29-30

These cards show key words that the children will encounter when working on the unit:

- words relating to belonging and the religions studied in this unit
- words to describe religious artefacts

Read through the word cards with the children to familiarise them with the key words of the unit. Ask which words the children have heard before and clarify any words that they don't understand.

Activities

- Cut out the cards and laminate them. Use them as often as possible when talking about ways in which people can belong to a particular religion, group or organisation.

- Encourage the children to match the word cards to the pictures in the Resource Gallery.
- Use the word cards for displays about 'Home, family and belonging'.
- Use the cards as a starting point to encourage the children to build their own word bank on 'Home, family and belonging'

I belong to ...

PAGE 31

This activity focuses on the children and the groups to which they belong. It is difficult for any child to understand about other people's families and belonging to a religious 'family' or faith, without having thought about the different groups to which they belong. There is no assumption here that every child will have links to a faith community. There is, however, the assumption that the children belong to many groups, such as the family home and their class. Some will also belong to other groups. This photocopiable sheet is a way of celebrating different ways of belonging and the relationships within each group. Complete the sheet following discussion, either in small or class groups, or during circle time.

Activities

- Talk to the children about the people in their families.
- Compare the class with the family to introduce the idea that the children belong to more than one group.
- Discuss with the children other groups they might belong to.
- Ask the children to draw themselves in the centre space and to represent the different groups they belong to on the activity sheet.
- Discuss and display the children's responses.

Belonging

PAGE 32

This activity sheet relates to the three religions which have been the focus for this chapter and can be used as a means of assessing how much the children have learned about the work on Christian, Jewish or Muslim families. The activity sheet shows Mary (a Christian); David (a Jew) and Safia (a Muslim).

Activities

- Cut out the pictures and let the children choose a character. Ask them to find the pictures associated with their chosen character. Help them to write about a special time for their chosen characters.
- Cut up the pictures and use them in a matching exercise to think about which pictures go with which religion.
- Use the pictures as 'Story Starters' and link them with other resources on the CD, for example, the picture of Mary can be linked with the pictures of the 'Easter Garden', 'Easter Eggs' and 'Hot cross buns'. Using the pictures, the children could make up a story about what Mary did at Easter.

Religion word cards

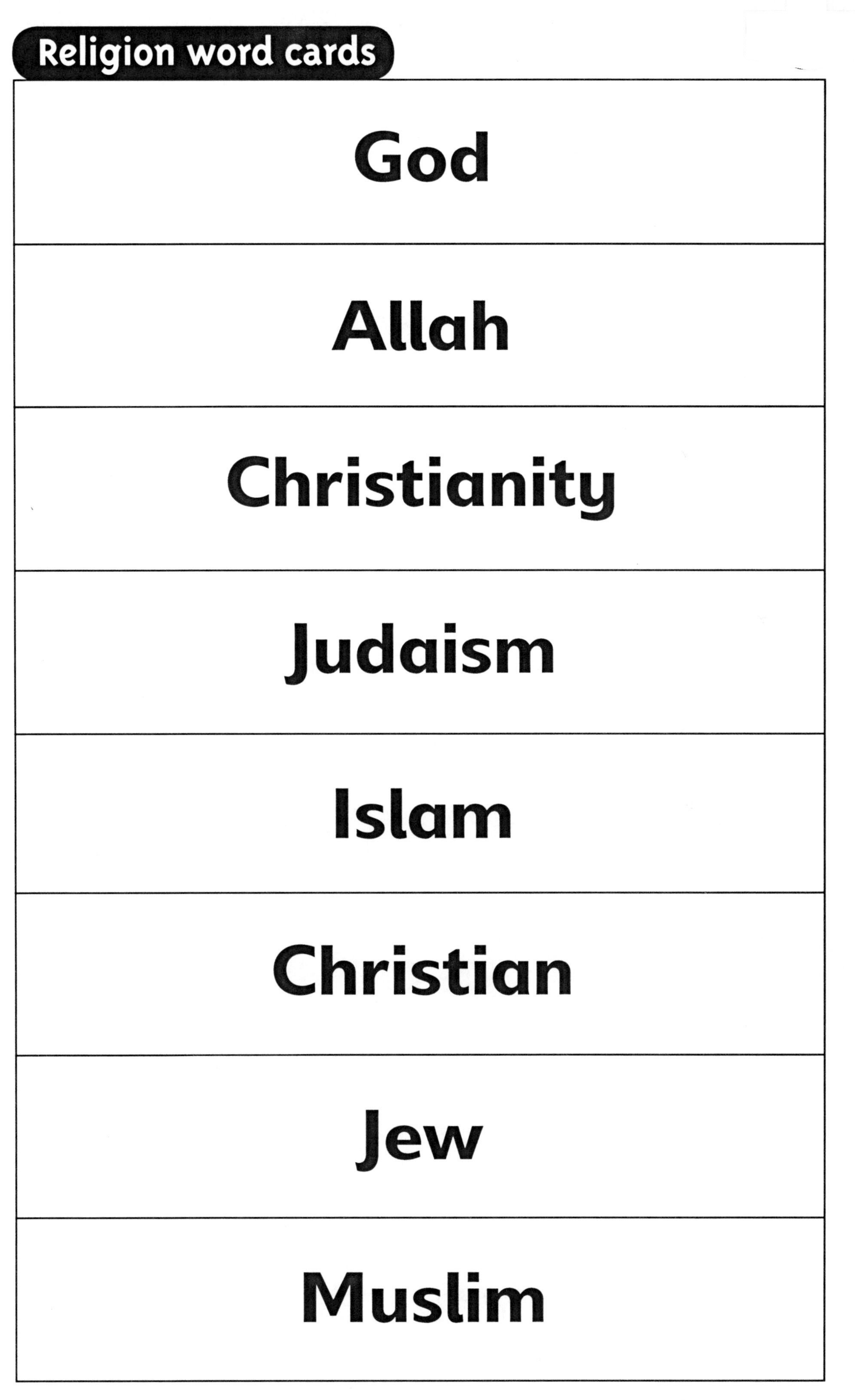

Belonging word cards

I belong to...

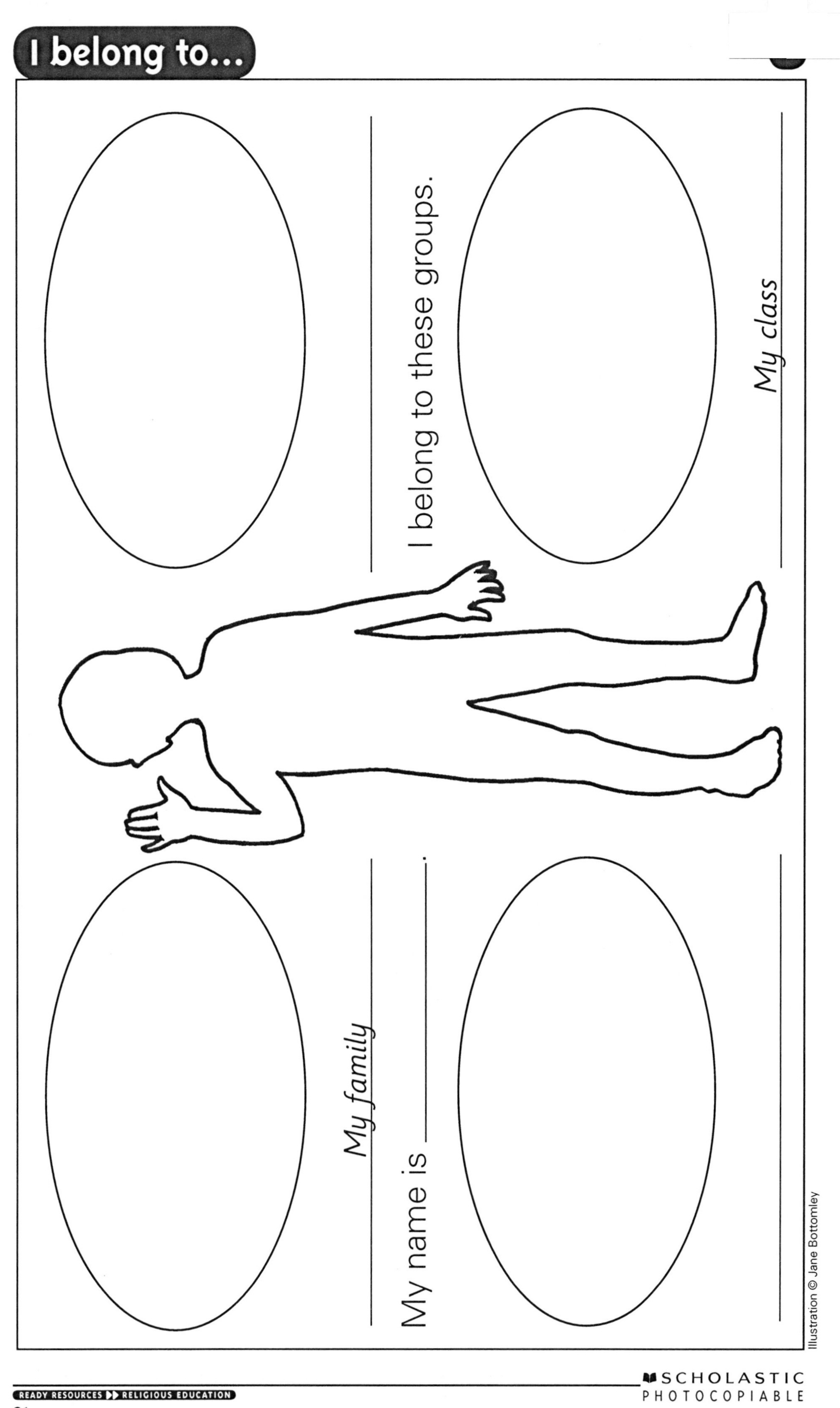
I belong to these groups.
My name is
My family
My class
Illustration © Jane Bottomley

Belonging

_____________________ is a Christian/ Jew/ Muslim.
In their home, you will see _____________________
____
____
A special time for _____________________ is
____
Mary
David
Safia
a Bible
a Qur'an
Shabbat candles
a Seder plate
a cross
prayer beads

CELEBRATIONS

Content and skills

This chapter addresses how and why people celebrate the rituals of baptism, Christmas, Easter, Passover, Ramadan and Divali. The theme of Celebrations is a common approach to teaching and learning in religious education at Key Stage 1. Through work on celebrations the children will encounter worship in the home as well as in the place of worship. They will learn about the beliefs and rituals of the family and of the faith community as well as the stories, special people and events which have given rise to these beliefs and rituals.

This chapter encourages the children to think about what it means to celebrate in a family and in a faith community. The ideas and activities will provide an insight in to what it means to celebrate within Christianity, Judaism and Islam. The chapter relates to the breadth of study in the non-statutory national framework for religious education which states that 'Christianity and at least one other principal religion should be taught at Key Stage 1'. It also relates to the framework's themes of celebrations, story and symbols. These are themes found in most locally agreed syllabuses for religious education, which form the legal requirement for teaching religious education.

The Resource Gallery for 'Celebrations' on the CD-ROM, together with the teacher's notes and photocopiable pages in this chapter, can be used to support teaching and learning about celebrations. The teacher's notes contain background information about the resources and include ways of using them as a whole class, for group work or as individuals. Some of the activities link with other areas of the curriculum, such as literacy and art and design. Wherever possible, the activities encourage the children to ask questions and develop an enquiring approach to their learning.

Resources on the CD-ROM

The resources include images of artefacts from Christianity, Judaism and Islam that you might find in a family home or in a place of worship. There are also photographs that show people both at home and in the church, synagogue and mosque. These resources serve to develop the children's understanding of celebration, and what it means to a religious family and faith community.

Photocopiable pages

The photocopiable pages in the book are also provided in PDF format on the CD-ROM and can be printed from there. They include:

- word cards containing essential vocabulary for the unit
- activity sheets on the stories of the Nativity and Passover
- activity sheets on celebrating Id-ul-Fitr and Divali
- an activity sheet on observing the phases of the Moon.

NOTES ON THE CD-ROM RESOURCES

BAPTISM

Certificate of baptism

This photograph shows a baptismal certificate for a baby girl, 'Mary-Ann', baptised at the age of three months. The certificate records the baby's name, the mother and father's names, the names of the three godparents, the place where the baptism took place and the name of the priest who baptised the baby. Parents who are Christians may choose to have their baby baptised as a way of welcoming the baby into the Christian family.

The family will take the baby to church, with the friends of the family and the godparents of the baby. This religious ritual or sacrament is called baptism, but many people will use the term 'christening' when the person to be baptised is a baby. People can be welcomed into the Christian church through baptism either as a baby or as an adult. See 'Baptismal font' (page 36) for further information.

During the baptismal service, the godparents promise that they will do their best to see that the child is brought up and cared for within the Christian family. The priest will say a blessing over the water in the baptismal font (photograph provided on the CD) and will pour some water over the baby's head, saying a blessing: 'In the name of the Father, Son and Holy Spirit'. This pouring of water is a symbol of washing or cleansing the baby for a new life as part of the Christian family. Then, after dipping his fingers into the water, the priest names the baby by making the sign of the cross on the baby's head.

Discussing the photograph

- Before using the resource, ask the children whether any of them have ever received a certificate – perhaps a certificate for good work at school, or for a sporting achievement. Discuss the reasons for receiving these certificates, the words on the certificates and the people who awarded them.
- Look at the baptismal certificate and identify the different parts – the name of the church, the date of birth and baptism and the official stamp of the church.
- Explain that baptism is a special time for Christians, and it is a time when a baby is welcomed into the Christian family.
- Talk to the children about the role of godparents. Godparents are people who agree to guide the baby and help the growing child to understand what it means to be part of the Christian family.

Activities

- Ask the children to bring in examples of certificates they have received, including baptism certificates. Share these with the class.
- Make photocopies of different types of certificates for display.
- Ask the children which 'groups' or 'families' they belong to. Support this activity with the use of photocopiable pages 31 and 32 ('I belong to...' and 'Belonging').
- Discuss the words of the promises that have to be made to join clubs such as the Brownies or Cubs. What do the promises mean?
- Discuss the promises made by the godparents to guide the baby. Ask the children who 'guides' them or gives them good advice – for example, parents and grandparents. Make a display of sketches of these special people, with speech bubbles showing some of the advice they have given.

Old christening dress, New christening dress, Baptism shell

The wearing of white dresses for baptism is a tradition based on the idea of 'white' being a symbol of 'purity'. The white gown is a symbol of the child's new life in the Christian family, which begins with the service of baptism.

The older of the two christening dresses is 74 years old and was handmade for baby Margaret's christening by her mother. The dress is made from cream silk and has hand-embroidered flowers around the hem. Many years later, the dress was then worn by

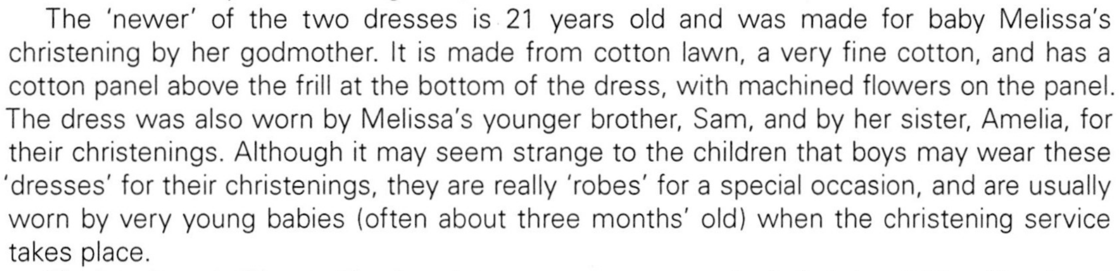

Margaret's two children, David and Helen. When David got married and had children, the dress was worn by his two daughters, Eleanor and Catherine.

The 'newer' of the two dresses is 21 years old and was made for baby Melissa's christening by her godmother. It is made from cotton lawn, a very fine cotton, and has a cotton panel above the frill at the bottom of the dress, with machined flowers on the panel. The dress was also worn by Melissa's younger brother, Sam, and by her sister, Amelia, for their christenings. Although it may seem strange to the children that boys may wear these 'dresses' for their christenings, they are really 'robes' for a special occasion, and are usually worn by very young babies (often about three months' old) when the christening service takes place.

The baptism shell is used by the priest to pour water over the baby's head. (See 'Baptismal candle' below for further information about the symbolism of the shell.)

Discussing the photographs

▶ Ask the children to describe what they can see in each of the pictures. Ask them to identify similarities and differences between the two dresses.
▶ Talk about the tradition of the baby wearing a white dress for the christening. Say that it is symbolic of the baby's 'new life' – becoming part of the family of the church.
▶ Talk about the histories of the 'old' and 'new' dresses; who made them, the materials used, the difference between 'hand' and 'machine' made.
▶ Ask the children whether any of them were christened. Did they wear a special christening robe or dress?

Activities

▶ Brainstorm the occasions when special clothes are worn.
▶ Make a 'family tree' to match each of the dresses in the pictures.
▶ Ask some of the children to bring in the christening robe worn at their baptism or the baptism of members of their family. If the robes are too precious, photographs could be displayed instead.
▶ Discuss other ways of welcoming a new baby into the community. For example, some Christian groups have services of dedication.

Baptismal candles

The resource shows baptismal candles and the boxes that contain them. These baptismal candles are white with a transfer of symbolic images – the cross, the dove and the shell. The cross is the symbol of Christianity and a sign that the person baptised is actually baptised into the Christian faith. During the service, the sign of the cross will be made on the head of the person baptised.

The dove is a symbol of peace and a reminder of the dove which, according to the Gospels, descended on the head of Jesus at his baptism in the River Jordan. The shell and the water are also symbolic of this event. When he was baptised, Jesus would have passed completely under the water. Babies today have water poured over their heads using a shell.

The candle is lit at the service to show that the baptised person has 'passed from darkness to light', that is into the light of God in their new, Christian life. The candle, like the water, is a powerful symbol of goodness and truth across the religions. Some churches will give the baby a smaller baptismal candle, often in a decorative box.

Discussing the photograph

▶ Talk together about the symbolism of candles and about times when candles are lit for special occasions such as at Christmas and on birthday cakes.
▶ Talk with the children about their feelings when candles are lit for special occasions. Focus on the contrasts between the darkness before the lighting of the candles and the tiny flame which manages to spread light into dark corners.
▶ Ask the children to identify and name the three symbols on the candle.
▶ Talk to the children about the symbolism of the cross, the shell and the water.

Activities

▶ Ask the children to describe times when the light of a small candle made them feel happy

and safe. Use the story *The Owl Who Was Afraid of the Dark* by Jill Tomlinson (Egmont Books) as a starting point for the discussion.

▶ Make a collage of baptismal candles to display on the classroom wall against a background of black paper. Talk about how the collage illustrates the theme 'from darkness into light'.

▶ Ask those children who have been baptised to bring in their baptismal candles. Talk about the similarities and differences between the candles.

▶ Invite a godparent to talk to the children about the promises they made when they became a godparent. Ask them what they do to try to be a good godparent to the child.

Baptismal font

This picture shows a stone baptismal font. This font has a lead liner in the top, which is waterproof, to contain the water that is poured into the font for baptism services. Water is usually poured into the font from a jug, and is then blessed for use in the baptism service. In the bottom of the font there is often a plughole, allowing any remaining 'blessed' water to pass directly into the ground. Where a metal liner is used, the water will be poured away.

Stone fonts may be decorated in many different ways. The font shown here is attractively but simply decorated, but some may have elaborate trees, symbolic of the Tree of Life, winding around their base.

Fonts are traditionally found near the entrance to the church as this is symbolic of a child being welcomed into the church building, and therefore the church family, at baptism. However, these days, many churches will conduct the baptism service from the front of the church, at the altar, and will use a portable font for this purpose. When this is the case, the font may be a simple metal bowl.

The use of water as a symbol of purity or newness of life dates back to early biblical times and was a practice used by Jews. Christians however, date their practice of baptism from the baptism of Jesus who was baptised in the River Jordan by John the Baptist before he started his ministry of teaching and healing. The story of Jesus' baptism is told in the Gospels of Matthew 3:13-17 and Luke 3:21-23. The stories tell of Jesus passing under the water and the spirit of God appearing like a dove. Jesus' baptism was as an adult and marked his new life of teaching and preaching. Although many Christians are baptised as babies in a church and at the font, other Christian traditions hold Believers' Baptism, which is the baptism of adults who are able to decide for themselves that they wish to follow Jesus' teaching and example and to live the Christian life. They therefore make the promises to do this for themselves. They may be baptised at the font but in some churches, in particular, Baptist and Pentecostal churches, they may be baptised in a baptismal pool, rather like a small swimming pool in the church. The person passes underneath the water as the priest or minister says a prayer over them and then they rise to 'a new life in Christ'. The water has 'washed them clean' of their past life and of any misdoings.

Discussing the photograph

▶ Talk with the children about how they feel when they have a bath or wash their hands. Ask them to identify words which describe their feelings.

▶ Show the children the picture of the font. Talk with them about the decoration on the font and ask them to guess where you might find this object.

▶ Using the resources 'Baptism certificate', 'Old christening dress', 'New christening dress', 'Baptism shell', and 'Baptismal candle' as successive clues, ask the children what special occasion might take place around this font.

Activities

▶ Visit a church and ask the vicar, priest or minister to explain how babies are welcomed into the Christian family in his or her church. If the church has a baptismal font, ask the children to draw a sketch of it.

▶ Role-play a baptism. Dress 'the baby' in a special white dress, choose a name for the child and choose parents and godparents. Ask the vicar or minister to 'baptise' the baby and say the blessings.

▶ Learn a song or write a new song to welcome a baby.

▶ Invite a mother with a young baby to speak to the children about how she cares for the baby, and what a baby needs to be well-cared for (emotional needs as well as practical).

▶ Discuss with the children gifts which they would like to give a new baby.
▶ Look at greetings cards sent at the birth of a new baby. Notice whether the greetings contain wishes for the new child. Ask the children to make greetings cards with appropriate wishes for the baby.
▶ Ask the children to bring in special gifts which they were given at the time of their baptism (with their parents' permission).
▶ Read the story about Jesus' baptism from a Children's Bible.
▶ Invite a person who was baptised as an adult to talk to the children about their experience.

CHRISTMAS

Advent ring with candles

The photograph shows an Advent ring or wreath. This consists of a wreath of fir, holly and ivy, with four red candles placed around the circle, and a white candle in the centre.

Advent is the period of four weeks leading up to Christmas, the word 'advent' coming from a Latin word meaning 'coming towards'. Advent is a period for 'looking forward' to the festival of Christmas. The Advent ring is used in churches, and sometimes in homes, as a way of preparing for the festival of Christmas. For Christians this marks the coming of God into this world in the person of Jesus – the word for this is 'incarnation', God born in human form, or 'in flesh'.

Beginning on Advent Sunday; the first Sunday in Advent, the first red candle is lit during the church service. The second candle is lit on the second Sunday in Advent and so on, until all four candles are lit. On Christmas Day, the day which marks the birth of Jesus, the white candle will also be lit. In Roman Catholic churches, pink and purple candles may be used instead of red candles.

The use of light as a symbol for the presence of God is an ancient and widespread practice. The presence of God is believed to bring light, truth and goodness into a world of darkness, a world where people do wrong and do not have knowledge and understanding of the truth about how they should behave and live their lives.

Discussing the photograph

▶ Talk with the children about their feelings when they are waiting for a special day, such as Christmas Day, to come.
▶ Ask the children to describe what they can see in the picture.
▶ Talk about the four red candles being lit on the four Sundays before Christmas and ask the children when they think the white candle might be lit.
▶ Discuss with the children how Christians make a wreath like this one when they are waiting for Christmas Day. Ask: *How might Christians feel each week as the candles are lit?*

Activities

▶ Make an Advent wreath for the classroom, using an evergreen such as fir or holly and ivy, and candles as shown in the resource.
▶ Light the Advent candles for 30 minutes each Monday in the weeks before Christmas. Tell a part of the Christmas story by the light of the candle, such as Mary and Joseph's journey to Bethlehem or the visit of the shepherds.
▶ Collect other ways of marking the days of Advent, such as an Advent candle with each day of December marked on it, or an Advent calendar.
▶ Make an Advent calendar for the classroom. First, collect a selection of pictures associated with the nativity story and then ask the children to select 24 of them for their calendar. Tell the children to include stars, angels

and a manger in their selection. The 25th and final picture will be the nativity scene. Next, stick the pictures spaced out on a piece of paper. Then superimpose a second piece with 25 numbered boxes over the first. Perforate the boxes so that they can be opened, one box each day, to reveal the picture behind the 'door'.

A Nativity scene

This photograph shows a Nativity scene from a triptych in a church. The central panel shows the stable scene with the baby Jesus in a manger and Mary next to her son. Above the baby's head is a group of angels, representing those who brought the good news of the birth of Jesus to the shepherds. To the left of the panel Joseph is shown and in the foreground one of the kings presenting gifts to the baby. The panel is rich in symbolism: the halos over the heads of Jesus, Mary and Joseph depict holiness; the traditional blue of Mary's robe reflects Mary's relation with 'heaven'; and the passion flower, to the bottom right, directs the thoughts of the viewer to the future death of Jesus on the cross.

The panel on the left shows two of the kings bringing gifts. The story of the visit of the kings is told in the Gospel of Matthew (2:1-12). The kings are sometimes referred to as astrologers as it is the sight of an unusual star that alerts them to the birth of this special child. There is also no reference to a specific number of kings in the Gospel, the number 'three' being a tradition.

The panel on the right depicts the visit of the shepherds to the baby, told in the Gospel of Luke (2:8-20). The Gospel tells that the shepherds learned about the birth of the baby by the angels who brought the good news as they were in the fields watching over their sheep. In the picture, the gifts brought by the shepherds are flowers, simple gifts of nature.

The visits of the kings or astrologers and the shepherds show that both rich and poor recognise the birth of Jesus as an important event and come to visit the child. In Christian teaching, the coming of God into the world in the person of Jesus, is a significant event for everyone – a universal event.

Discussing the artwork

- Look at the centre panel first. Ask the children to identify the characters they recognise.
- Discuss with the children why the artist has painted halos around the heads of some of the characters. What do they think the artist was trying to show?
- Discuss the characters in the side panels and the gifts which they have brought to Jesus. What gifts would they have taken to the baby?
- Explain that Christians believe that Jesus was a gift from God to the world. Why might Christians believe that Jesus was a special gift?

Activities

- Give each group of children a beautifully decorated box. Ask each child to place or draw a gift for a baby in the box. At circle time, ask each group to share what is in their box and why those gifts would be appropriate for a new baby.
- Using the centre panel, recreate the scene in class. Choose one child to be Mary. Ask the rest of the class to 'direct' her as to how to sit and where to place her hands. Choose a boy to be Joseph, with the rest of the class directing him. Repeat this process with the kings and with the angels.
- Take a picture of the scene with a digital camera and compare it with the original.
- Discuss the feelings of the individual characters.
- Project the Nativity image onto a whiteboard. Provide some Christmas cards and ask the children to sort the cards to match the different parts of the story.
- Ask the children to choose the part of the nativity story that they like best. Let them make Christmas cards with that image on the front. Ask them to draw a gift for Jesus inside the card.

Video: Why Christmas is a special time

The video presents a child who describes what happens at Christmas and why it is special in his home and faith community.

The boy explains that at home, Christmas is a time to decorate the house, put up a Christmas tree and give presents and cards to one another. It is also a time for a special family meal – a time

for fun and enjoyment. At church, Christmas is a time for nativity plays, carols and stories about the birth of Jesus. There is also a big candle which represents the light of God coming down to the earth in the person of Jesus.

Discussing the video

▶ Discuss the ways in which the children celebrate Christmas, or spend the Christmas holiday.
▶ Talk about the number of different things the child on the video does at Christmas – both at home and in church.
▶ Discuss the importance of candles and light at Christmas time and the meaning of light.

Activities

▶ Make a sketch of the child for a collage, with bubbles around him depicting the different Christmas activities.
▶ Invite visitors such as teaching assistants and parents into the classroom to be interviewed by the children about how they spend Christmas. Some may be religious, others not so. Use the video as a model for preparing the interviews.
▶ Look at the resources showing the Advent Ring and the Nativity scene (see above). Discuss the feelings of Christians during Advent and later, when Christmas arrives.

Audio: Christmas carol (Away in a Manger)

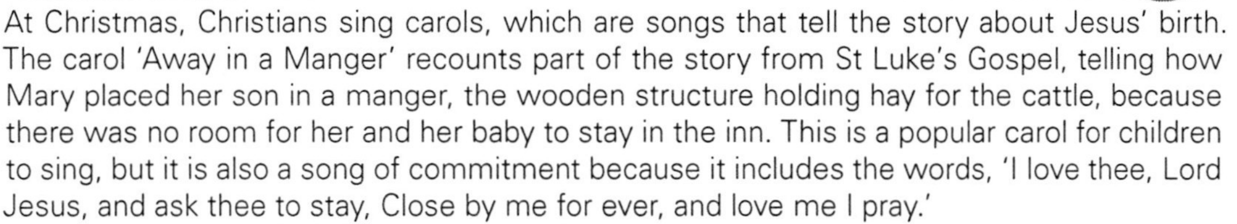

At Christmas, Christians sing carols, which are songs that tell the story about Jesus' birth. The carol 'Away in a Manger' recounts part of the story from St Luke's Gospel, telling how Mary placed her son in a manger, the wooden structure holding hay for the cattle, because there was no room for her and her baby to stay in the inn. This is a popular carol for children to sing, but it is also a song of commitment because it includes the words, 'I love thee, Lord Jesus, and ask thee to stay, Close by me for ever, and love me I pray.'

Other carols retell different parts of the nativity story. For example, 'O Little Town of Bethlehem' is a reminder of the place where Jesus was born; 'While Shepherds Watched their Flocks by Night' tells of the shepherds receiving the good news of Jesus' birth from the angels (see Luke 2:8-20); and 'We Three Kings' tells about the visit of the kings to the new-born baby (see Matthew 2:1-12).

Discussing the song

▶ Listen to the song with the children. Ask them if they know what it is called and whether they have sung or heard it before.
▶ Ask the children to describe the pictures in their minds when they sing this carol.
▶ Read out the lyrics to the children. Talk to the children about the meanings of some of the words and phrases, for example, 'crib'; 'away in a manger'.
▶ Discuss with the children what type of a song they think this is. Is it meant to make Mary happy, or to wake up the baby? This carol is actually like a lullaby, sung to comfort the baby and send it to sleep.

Activities

▶ Collect Christmas cards and divide them into different groups: those showing the nativity story and seasonal or traditional cards (for example, with robins or Christmas trees).
▶ Try to find cards that depict nativity scenes that can be linked to Christmas carols.
▶ Give each group of children one card which tells part of the nativity story. Each group has to learn a carol which matches the picture on the card. The groups sing their carols, telling the stories about the birth of Jesus. Use this work as the basis of a class assembly.

EASTER

Jesus' last supper

The picture shows a replica painting of Leonardo Da Vinci's painting of The Last Supper. The painting is situated within a church, behind the main altar. It was painted and presented to the church by a member of the congregation in 1914. The painting shows Jesus in the centre,

presiding over the last meal that he shared with his disciples: Peter, Andrew, James (the Greater), John, Thomas, James (the Less), Jude, Philip, Bartholomew, Matthew, Simon, and Judas Iscariot. In this painting, there is one long table, but other artists have painted a three-sided table which groups the disciples more closely. Tradition suggests that the three-sided arrangement was more in keeping with practices at the time of Jesus.

The story of the Last Supper is told in the Gospels: Matthew 26:17-29; Mark 14:12-25; Luke 22:7-38. It was the time of the Passover and Jesus told two of his disciples to go into the city of Jerusalem and to follow a man carrying a jar of water. The man would lead them to a house where they would prepare a Passover meal in an upper room. At the meal there are three key events. Firstly, Jesus says that one of the disciples will betray him and a dispute breaks out amongst the disciples as to who this might be. This painting seems to reflect this dispute. Secondly, Jesus, like every Jew celebrating the Passover meal, says blessings over the wine and the bread, but Jesus gives a special meaning to this, saying that the wine and the bread are like his blood and his body. It is this which initiates the Christian celebration of Holy Communion. Thirdly, Jesus says that one of his disciples will disown him. Peter says that he would never deny that he knows Jesus, but before the cock crows at dawn, Peter does deny Jesus three times.

Discussing the picture

- Ask the children to look at the picture and to identify which person might be Jesus.
- Talk about the other people in the painting and the feelings suggested by the position of their bodies. Discuss whether this looks like an ordinary meal with friends.
- Explain that this painting shows Jesus' last supper – an important event that is remembered by Christians.
- Make links between the painting which shows a meal and how Christians commemorate this meal by sharing bread and wine in Holy Communion.

Activities

- Read a simplified account of Jesus' last supper with his disciples from a Children's Bible.
- Print and laminate a copy of the picture for each group of pupils. Stick the picture on a large piece of sugar paper, with speech and thought bubbles drawn from the main characters in the picture. Ask the children to fill in the thought and speech bubbles. Create an art gallery of all the pictures, displayed around the class. Discuss and compare the statements in the bubbles.
- Using 'happy', 'sad' and 'angry' faces, create a 'feelings map', either of the painting itself or of the story of the Last Supper.
- Look at other paintings showing the Last Supper and compare them with this. Note the similarities and differences in how they show the same story.
- Set a table with some of the foods which might have been eaten at the Last Supper. These would include wine (red grape juice); bread (unleavened bread or bread without yeast – such as pitta bread); probably dates and olives (which are products of Israel).

Hot cross buns, Easter eggs

Hot cross buns and Easter eggs are reminders of the Good Friday and Easter Day stories, and the Christian celebrations of these two days. Hot cross buns are traditionally eaten on Good Friday. The cross on the top of the bun is a reminder of the cross on which Jesus died. The buns contain spices which are reminders of the spices used to anoint the body of Jesus. The basket of hot cross buns is placed on a purple cloth – the liturgical colour of Lent. The basket of Easter eggs is shown on a white background – gold and white are the liturgical colours used for celebrations. In contrast with the hot cross buns which symbolise death, the eggs are a symbol of new life.

For Christians at Easter time, the symbols of new life signify the new life following the resurrection of Jesus. In the Orthodox Church, Christians will hard boil and dye eggs for breakfast on Easter morning. In some churches, hard boiled eggs will be distributed after the service and children will hit each others' eggs until one of the eggs cracks, symbolising the breaking open of the tomb and new life emerging. Most children will recognise, and enjoy, chocolate Easter eggs and some families will have an Easter egg hunt, with eggs hidden around the garden. The picture shows two large, commercially

produced eggs and smaller painted eggs. These are chicken's eggs, with beautiful designs painted by hand.

Discussing the photographs

- Talk to the children about times when special food might be eaten to remember someone or something (such as birthday, wedding or Christening cakes, or eating haroset at Passover as a way of remembering the cement used to build new homes).
- Look at the picture of the hot cross buns and ask the children if they can recognise a symbol that they might have seen before (a cross).
- Look at the picture of the Easter eggs and discuss with the children the links between eggs and new life – for example, birds such as chickens and ducks and even crocodiles are born from eggs.
- Ask the children about different types of Easter eggs that they have seen.
- Talk about other special foods that the children may eat at Easter time.

Activities

- Make and taste some hot cross buns.
- Collect together artefacts and picture resources which show different types of crosses in different settings. For example, use 'Three crosses' and 'Crucifix' from Chapter One. Ask the children to notice and describe the different materials used to make crosses.
- Paint hard-boiled eggs. Edible food dyes could be used if the eggs are to be eaten, or use paints or felt-tipped pens for more intricate designs. Wipe the eggs with oil to give a shiny finish.
- Make a collection of eggs and other symbols of new life – for example, bulbs, flowers, pictures of baby animals. Display this collection on a white, yellow or gold backcloth as a symbol of celebration.

Easter garden

Many churches, during the period of Easter, have an Easter garden on display, either inside the church, in the entrance porch or in the grounds. This photograph shows a typical example of an Easter garden. Easter gardens usually display a 'tomb'. This garden depicts an open tomb reminiscent of the empty tomb after Jesus' resurrection on Easter Day. The stone slab on which the body would have been placed is visible and some 'tombs' have pieces of white cloth inside to represent the burial robes remaining after the resurrection. The path suggests the way out of the tomb. Three crosses can be seen – the crosses of those who were crucified with Jesus, while the spring flowers in the foreground symbolise the joy of Easter Day.

Discussing the photograph

- Ask the children to identify the different parts of the Easter garden – the three crosses, the tomb, the path and the flowers.
- Focus on the gravel path. Ask the children where they think the path starts and where it ends.
- Together, talk about the happy and sad parts of the garden.

Activities

- Use the picture of the Easter Garden to tell a simplified version of the death and resurrection of Jesus. For example: 'Jesus was crucified on a cross, and his body was put in a tomb. The disciples were sad. When Jesus' friends went to the tomb, an angel told them that Jesus was no longer there, he had risen. The disciples and friends were happy.'
- Make a list of the things needed to make an Easter garden for the classroom. For example: twigs for crosses, a flower pot to

represent the tomb (or a papier mâché tomb with a round stone to cover the opening until Easter Day when the stone can be rolled away), gravel for the path and flowers to show the joy of Easter Day.

- Discuss the types of flowers which could be chosen for the garden. They could be chosen because of their colours or for their special meanings. Ideas include forget-me-nots and rosemary for remembrance.
- Learn an Easter Day song. These could include 'Jesus in the garden' from *Come and Praise 2* (BBC) or 'H'ristos anesti' from Light the Candles! (Cambridge University Press).
- Invite a vicar or minister to talk to the children about what happens in their church on Easter Day.
- Visit a church to look at their Easter Garden.

Video: Celebrating Easter in church

Christians celebrate Easter at home and in church. The festival of Easter includes Good Friday, Easter Saturday and Easter Day. The video shows a Christian child describing what takes place in her church at Easter. She explains that the festival is a time when Christians remember the death of Jesus and how he rose again. In her church, this 'new life' is symbolised by lighting a big Easter candle. It is a happy time for singing special hymns and for getting Easter Eggs.

Discussing the video

- Talk to the children about the two events Christians remember at Easter – the death of Jesus on Good Friday and the time of celebrating new life on Easter Day.
- Remind the children of some of the resources already seen which are symbols of these days such as hot cross buns and Easter eggs.
- Discuss with the children other signs of new life. For example, bulbs growing in the spring, trees bursting into bud, new lambs and other animals.

Activities

- Read some stories about changes in nature such as *The Very Hungry Caterpillar* by Eric Carle (Puffin). Talk to the children about the natural changes 'from death to life.'
- Visit a church to look at an example of a large Easter or Paschal Candle. Look for the symbols of the nails and the transfer showing the year on the candle.
- Invite two or more Christian parents or teaching assistants to speak to the children about how Easter is celebrated in their churches.
- Share some Easter eggs!

PASSOVER

Seder plate and matzot, Seder plate ready for Passover

The photograph 'Seder plate and matzot' shows a Seder plate, three matzot and a bowl of salt water, all items to be found on the table for the Seder meal – the celebratory meal which takes place in each Jewish family's home at the beginning of the festival of Passover.

The Hebrew word in the middle of the Seder plate is the word 'Pesach', the Hebrew word for 'Passover'. The Hebrew letters are written and read from right to left. On this Seder plate, the items are identified in Hebrew and in English, but on many Seder plates, there is a transliteration of the Hebrew word, for example 'maror' for 'bitter herbs'.

The photograph 'Seder plate ready for Passover' shows the plate filled with the symbolic foods: (clockwise from top) shankbone, haroset, horseradish roots (for bitter herbs), parsley, salt water, roasted egg. Each item on the Seder plate is a reminder of the time when the Jews, then referred to as Hebrews, were slaves in Egypt and how God through Moses, led them out of slavery in Egypt to freedom.

The bitter herbs, or 'maror', are used as a reminder of the bitter times in slavery, (horseradish is usually used to represent this). The vegetable, 'karpas' (usually parsley) is dipped in the bowl of salt water to remember how, in the biblical story, hyssop (a herb) was dipped in lamb's blood and smeared on the doorposts of the homes of the Hebrew people the night before they left Egypt. That night, the firstborn in every Hebrew home was safe, while the firstborn in every Egyptian home, human and animal, died. The shank bone of a lamb, 'zeroa', is a reminder of the roasted lamb eaten the night before the escape from Egypt. The egg, a 'roasted' egg or 'betzah', is a hard-boiled egg which is then roasted in an oven or, more generally, over a naked flame until it looks burnt. It is a symbol of the burning of the sacrifices made in the Temple, but more commonly is thought of as a symbol of new life. The egg on the Seder plate is not eaten, but many families begin the meal with hard-boiled egg as part of the first course of the meal. 'Haroset' is a mixture of grated apple, nuts and cinnamon, mixed together with wine. The colour is a reminder of the mortar used by the slaves to build the pyramids, but its sweet taste softens the bitter memories of slavery.

The matzot are a reminder of the 'bread of affliction', the bread eaten by the Hebrews when they were slaves in Egypt. It is also a reminder of unleavened bread – bread without yeast, because the Hebrews left Egypt in a hurry and did not have time to wait for the bread to rise. The bowl of salt water represents the tears and the sweat of the slaves.

Everyone in the Jewish family will have a taste of each of the symbolic foods on the Seder plate as the story of Moses and the escape from Egypt is recounted. Following this ritual retelling of the story, there will be a family meal with songs, which last late into the night.

Discussing the photograph

- Look at the Seder plates and ask the children to identify the items which can be seen in the pictures.
- Compare the two photographs and ask the children to match the pictures with the foods illustrated on photocopiable page 55.
- Talk about each of the items with the children and explain that all these special foods remind Jews of the time when Hebrews were freed from slavery in Egypt. Ask them to think of other foods that remind people of special times.

Activities

- Taste some of the foods seen in the picture such as horseradish (creamed horseradish in a jar), parsley and matzot (boxed matzot can be bought from supermarkets). If possible, bring in horseradish roots so that the children can feel and smell it.
- Read the story of Moses on photocopiable page 77, 'Moses leads the slaves to freedom'.
- Begin to make links between parts of the story and the foods on the Seder plate. For example, the bitter herbs and the bitter times when the Hebrews were slaves; the salt water and the sweat and tears of the slaves.
- Watch a video about a Jewish family celebrating Passover. For example, watch: *Celebrations* (BBC Worldwide Ltd).
- Use this resource with photocopiable page 55 'Remembering Passover' to pair the items on the Seder plate with the story of Moses and the Passover.

Hunt for leaven

This photograph shows one of the family activities or rituals which takes place before the festival of Passover begins. During Passover the family will eat no food containing a raising agent such as yeast, and no bread will be eaten during the festival. Instead, the family will eat matzot, cracker-like biscuits. This is to remember how the Hebrews had no time to let their bread rise before leaving Egypt. Many foods contain a raising agent and all these are removed from the house in the days before the festival. Each room in the house is cleaned thoroughly so that nothing with yeast in it remains. The night before Passover begins, one of the parents will hide pieces of bread, usually in plastic bags around the house, and the children, with the help of a candle and a feather will 'hunt for the leaven'. When they have found every piece of bread, these will be taken outside the house and burned. A prayer is said, asking God to forgive the family if any trace of leaven remains.

Discussing the photograph

- Discuss with the children how bread is made, and how it rises with the yeast in it.
- Recall the special meal that was prepared by the Hebrew slaves to eat before they left Egypt in a hurry.

▶ Talk to the children about all the things that they eat which contain a raising agent such as bread, cakes and biscuits.

Activities

▶ Identify all the common foods that contain a raising agent. Make a display or collage of all the things that a Jewish child could not eat during Passover.
▶ Look for some recipes from Jewish cookbooks, or some ingredients from the Kosher section of local supermarkets. Jewish families will substitute matzah meal for self raising flour.
▶ Invite a Jew to talk to the children about the foods that can and cannot be eaten during Passover.
▶ Ask the children to 'interview' family members about special times when they spring clean their houses.
▶ Hide some pieces of bread, wrapped in plastic bags, around the classroom and choose some children to find the pieces. Challenge the children to ask key questions to try to find the bread, with the rest of the class responding and providing clues where necessary.

RAMADAN

Preparing breakfast during Ramadan, Eating during Ramadan

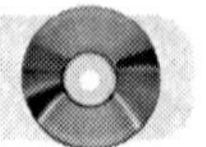

During the month of Ramadan, Muslim adults do not eat or drink during daylight hours. It is a time when Muslims change their routine habits and the automatic pleasures of eating and drinking in order to turn their attention to their spiritual life. It is also a time to remember those people in the world who do not have enough to eat.

The month of Ramadan begins when the new moon, signifying the beginning of the month, is seen in the sky. Muslims follow a lunar calendar, so the month of Ramadan moves forward by ten or eleven days each year. Consequently, the times when the fasting begins and ends varies according to the time of year in which Ramadan occurs. At the time of writing, Ramadan occurs during October to November, with dawn breaking late and the sun setting early in the day. Consequently, the hours of fasting are fewer. However, in a few years' time, when Ramadan occurs in August, dawn will break earlier in the day and the sun will set later, so creating a longer period of fasting. It can also be more onerous to go without food and water in the summer rather than the autumn months.

Children, the elderly, the sick, and pregnant women are not required to fast. If a person inadvertently breaks the fast, or if a person is ill and has to eat, then the days of fasting can be made up on subsequent days. Children should not be encouraged to think of fasting as a punishment. Although it is one of the five requirements for a Muslim, it is a time when Muslims speak of feeling closer to Allah, and to members of their family when they share meals together and meet at the mosque to pray.

The family will rise early, before dawn, and have their breakfast before the hours of fasting begin. The first picture shows the family preparing a nourishing breakfast which will sustain them throughout the day. Although children are not required to fast, many will wish to participate with the rest of the family. Some children will fast for part of the day to share in the experience. The family will not eat again until after sunset. Some families will go to the mosque to pray in the late afternoon or early evening and break the fast with the Muslim community, often by eating dates and drinking water. Afterwards they will eat an evening meal.

The second picture shows a family eating together. They have their hands raised in supplication or prayer to Allah before eating. The meal shared will be a 'halal' meal – that is, any meat will have been bought from a halal butcher (where the animal will have been killed according to Muslim tradition). Muslims do not eat pork nor pork products, or shellfish.

Discussing the photographs

▶ Tell the children about the festival of Ramadan, and explain that these two photographs show important times during Ramadan – before the fast begins (before sunrise) and breaking the fast (after sunset).
▶ Talk to the children about how the family will have their breakfast before dawn, and that this time will change every year, depending on the time of year in which Ramadan falls.

▶ Discuss with the children what time they usually have breakfast and what they eat at breakfast time.
▶ Talk together about people in the world who do not have enough to eat.
▶ Look at the second picture showing the family eating during Ramadan. Discuss why they might have their hands raised. Do the children know any prayers people might say before eating food?

Activities

▶ Make a timetable of the times when the children in the class eat their meals and snacks.
▶ Using a timetable that predicts the sunrise and sunset times in a week, make a timetable of a Muslim boy or girl's meal times during Ramadan. (The BBC weather website www.bbc.co.uk/weather gives sunrise and sunset times as part of its five-day forecast.)
▶ Plan a nourishing breakfast for a Muslim child, remembering that he or she would not be able to eat pork.
▶ Invite the children to describe or draw their favourite meals.
▶ Invite a Muslim to speak to the children about a typical day's meals in a Muslim household.
▶ Taste some dates – it is a tradition to break the fast by eating dates, before having a proper meal.

Zakat box, Video: What is Zakat?

Zakat is one of the Five Pillars of Islam. The Five Pillars of Islam are:

1. The Shahadah – Muslims should recite the Shahadah, a statement of Muslim belief
2. Salah – Muslims should pray five times a day
3. Zakat – Muslims should give zakat, money collected for the poor
4. Sawm – Muslims should fast during Ramadan
5. Hajj – Muslims should go on a pilgrimage to Makkah

Zakat is a payment of money, made by every Muslim each year. The money is used to support the poor and needy locally, nationally and internationally. Although commonly thought of as charity, the importance of zakat is the effect it has on the giver. The prescribed giving to others is an act of worship and is seen as having a spiritual effect. It is also a way of 'purifying' one's own wealth. Ramadan is a time to remember others, and children will often collect zakat during this period.

The picture shows a box produced by the Muslim community to encourage young children to collect their pennies for zakat.

Awareness of the money that is given to charities, on occasions such as Red Nose Day and Children in Need, has involved younger pupils in schools in donating time, effort and funds, and this makes it easier for all pupils in schools to understand the concept of giving as zakat in the Muslim community.

In the video, a Muslim mother and son, talk about what zakat is about and emphasise that it is a time to think about others and to think about how lucky they are.

Discussing the photograph and video

▶ Discuss times when the school or class has collected money for charities.
▶ Ask the children which charities they think are important to support – for example, charities for children or for animals.
▶ Discuss with the children how they feel when they have given some money to help another person.
▶ Explain to the children that zakat is often collected at the end of Ramadan – a special time for Muslims, when they are encouraged to think about people who are poor and in need.
▶ Look at the picture of the zakat box and ask the children if they have also used special boxes like this to collect for charity.
▶ Ask the children to think about the things that they are grateful for, and to think about others who might be in need. Help them to learn about developing countries and what their schools might be like in comparison to their own.

Activities

▶ Make a collection box for the children to use to collect for a chosen charity.
▶ Invite someone from the children's chosen charity to come to the school to receive

the money raised. Ask him or her to talk to the children about how the charity uses these donations to help others.

▶ Ask a Muslim to speak to the children about how collecting zakat at Ramadan makes them feel.

Id-ul-Fitr cards

Id-ul-Fitr is the day which marks the end of fasting after the month of Ramadan. It is a joyful occasion when families will wear their best clothes, go to the mosque for prayers, have special celebratory meals with their families and friends and give greetings cards and presents. The picture shows some Id greetings cards. The cards display a range of designs including flower and leaf designs, geometric patterns, images of mosques and minarets (including the Ka'bah in Makkah) and Arabic script. The special greeting is 'Id Mubarak' meaning 'Id blessings' or 'a happy Id'.

Discussing the photograph

▶ As a whole group, talk about the special times when the children send greetings cards to their friends.

▶ Talk to the children about the celebration of Id at the end of Ramadan.

▶ Look at the range of designs on the Id cards. Ask the children why they may think certain pictures or symbols are special.

Activities

▶ Use photocopiable page 56, 'Design an Id-ul-Fitr card' to create a collection of Id cards for a class display.

▶ Learn the Id greeting: 'Id Mubarak'.

▶ Gather the children's own cards and collect other Id cards to make a display on the theme of 'Celebrating Id-ul-Fitr'. This can be part of a display about Ramadan.

▶ Have an Id party with special food (there must not be any pork products). Muslims might have a sweet lamb curry and sweets such as those bought from Asian food shops.

▶ Make uncooked coconut sweets for the party – see the recipe resource, page 58 for Divali.

DIVALI

Rama and Sita

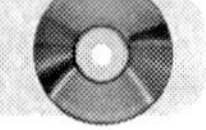

Divali is a Hindu New Year festival which occurs in the autumn – the precise date changing each year. Divali is celebrated in different ways in different parts of India, but in this country most Hindu communities will retell the story of Rama and Sita, and worship the goddess Lakshmi, the goddess of wealth and prosperity (for further information, see 'Lakshmi' below'). This is a celebration of Rama's rescue of Sita after she was captured by Ravana, the ten-headed demon.

This picture shows Lord Rama, the central figure with the bow, and his wife, Sita, the figure on his left. The figure on Lord Rama's right is that of his brother, Lakshman, also shown with a bow and arrows. At Lakshman's feet is the Monkey General, Hanuman, who helped Lord Rama to find Sita and to fight Ravana. The story of Lord Rama and Sita is told on photocopiable page 80 in Chapter 4 'Special books and stories'.

During Divali, Hindu families send each other Divali cards, give each other gifts and light divas, the small clay lights. In the business world, new accounts books for a new financial year are started at Divali.

Discussing the picture

▶ Invite the children to talk about the characters shown in the

picture. What are the three things they think are most important in the picture?

- ▶ Discuss with the children how they could tell that Rama is the most important person in the picture? (The radiant light around him; he is the central figure; his blue colour indicates that he is a god.)
- ▶ Ask the children if they can spot the clues which tell them that Rama and his brother Lakshmana like hunting?
- ▶ Tell the children about Rama and Sita, and talk about the different characters in the picture.

Activities

- ▶ Tell the story of Rama and Sita using the picture and photocopiable page 80 'Rama and Sita' (Chapter 4 'Special books and stories').
- ▶ Ask the children to retell the story of Rama and Sita in their own words or pictures using the picture as a prompt.
- ▶ Role-play the different scenes in the story. For example, Sita sees a deer in the forest and asks Rama to get it for her, Lakshman draws a circle around the hut, Ravana asks for food and so on.
- ▶ Ask the children to identify the good characters (such as Rama and Hanuman) and the bad character (Ravana).
- ▶ Focus on Hanuman, the Monkey General as the 'hero' who helps Rama to find Sita again. Imagine that Rama is going to make a speech to thank Hanuman. What would he say? Role-play the scene and make a garland for 'Rama' to place around Hanuman's neck.

Celebrating Divali, Diva lamps, Aum symbol

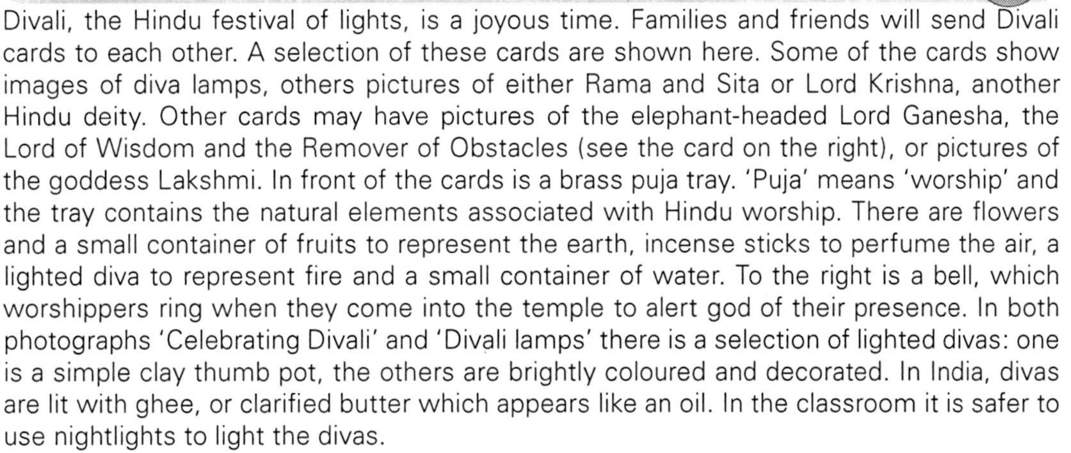

Divali, the Hindu festival of lights, is a joyous time. Families and friends will send Divali cards to each other. A selection of these cards are shown here. Some of the cards show images of diva lamps, others pictures of either Rama and Sita or Lord Krishna, another Hindu deity. Other cards may have pictures of the elephant-headed Lord Ganesha, the Lord of Wisdom and the Remover of Obstacles (see the card on the right), or pictures of the goddess Lakshmi. In front of the cards is a brass puja tray. 'Puja' means 'worship' and the tray contains the natural elements associated with Hindu worship. There are flowers and a small container of fruits to represent the earth, incense sticks to perfume the air, a lighted diva to represent fire and a small container of water. To the right is a bell, which worshippers ring when they come into the temple to alert god of their presence. In both photographs 'Celebrating Divali' and 'Divali lamps' there is a selection of lighted divas: one is a simple clay thumb pot, the others are brightly coloured and decorated. In India, divas are lit with ghee, or clarified butter which appears like an oil. In the classroom it is safer to use nightlights to light the divas.

The 'Aum' symbol is the symbol of Hinduism. Sometimes this is written as 'Om'. 'Aum' is the most sacred sound representing the divine. If it is sounded correctly, with the lips closed on the long final 'm' sound, the reverberation of this mantra will be experienced through the face and head.

Discussing the photographs

- ▶ Talk about the items in the photographs – the cards, puja tray and diva lamps.
- ▶ Tell the children that these items are used when celebrating the festival of Divali. Ask them to think of other special occasions when similar items are used.
- ▶ Talk with the children about the different times when they send greetings cards and what greeting is written on those cards – for example, 'Happy Christmas' and 'Happy Birthday'.
- ▶ Talk with the children about the different times when they light special candles or lights. Ask them to think about why the lights are special at these times.
- ▶ Tell the children about the 'Aum' symbol, which is a special symbol in Hinduism.

Activities

- ▶ Make Divali cards, decorating the front of the card with aspects of the story of Lord Rama and Sita. For example, the card could show Rama and Sita, Hanuman the Monkey King, or brightly coloured divas.
- ▶ Make and decorate some divas, using clay or Plasticine. Use a nightlight to light the divas. Emphasise safety matters and never leave the candles unattended.

▶ Tell the children the story of 'Lakshmi and the Poor Washerwoman' (see notes for 'Lakshmi' below). If possible, tell the story by the light of divas.
▶ Set up a shrine in the classroom similar to one which a Hindu family might have in their home. You will need: a red table covering, a picture of Rama and Sita or a picture of Lakshmi, laminated or backed with card and standing upright; a small metal tray with a diva, some flowers, a dish of fruits such as sultanas, a small dish of water, incense sticks and a bell.

Lakshmi

This resource shows Lakshmi, the goddess of wealth and good fortune who is especially worshipped at Divali. As Divali is a New Year festival, Hindus hope that Lakshmi will bring them wealth and good fortune in the coming year. Businessmen draw the symbol of Lakshmi in the front of their new account books in the hope that the coming year will bring them wealth and prosperity.

Lakshmi is shown as being many handed, which is a symbol of her powers as a goddess. She is also shown seated on a lotus flower – a beautiful and delicate flower, which grows up from the murky waters. Lakshmi is often depicted holding a lotus flower in her upper hands or with a left hand outstretched of which coins are shown falling from this hand. At Divali, a story is often told about Lakshmi:

Every Divali, the king gave his wife a beautiful present to show how much he loved her. One Divali, he gave her a wonderful pearl necklace. The Queen was very pleased with her gift. That night, she went to bathe in the river, and as she bathed, a large black crow picked up her necklace and flew off. He dropped the necklace in the basket of a poor washerwoman. The washerwoman was so poor that Poverty was her constant companion, but she was honest, and ran all the way to the king's palace to return the necklace. The king promised her anything she wanted as a reward. The poor washerwoman asked that no one in the kingdom should have lights in their home on this Divali. This was a strange thing to ask, but the king agreed and made an order that no one should light any divas in their homes.

The poor washerwoman went to the market and bought all the divas she could afford. Then she went home and lit a diva in every corner of her house.

When Lakshmi came to bless all the homes in the kingdom, there were no lights to welcome her. Then in the distance, she saw one house ablaze with lights. She knocked on the door and asked to be let in. The washerwoman called through the letterbox, 'Lakshmi, I will let you in, but only if you promise to stay with me for seven years!' Lakshmi agreed.
Just then, the washerwoman heard Poverty trying to get out of the back door. 'If Lakshmi comes in, there will be no room for me,' cried Poverty. 'Please let me out!' The washerwoman agreed to unlock the door – but only if Poverty promised not to return for seven years. Poverty promised and left the house. Lakshmi, the goddess of wealth and prosperity stayed with the poor washerwoman for seven happy years!

Discussion points

▶ Look at the image of Lakshmi. Ask the children to describe what they notice about her. Does Lakshmi look kind or scary?
▶ Discuss with the children what being a goddess of 'wealth' and 'good fortune' might mean. Does 'good fortune' always mean having lots of money?
▶ Talk to the children about the things different people might ask for. Would adults and children ask Lakshmi for the same things?

Activities

▶ Make a large collage of Lakshmi using red tissue paper for her clothes and lots of gold jewellery.
▶ Tell the story of 'Lakshmi and the Poor Washerwoman' (see above). Role-play this story or draw pictures to illustrate it.
▶ Make a list of all the things the children would like to ask Lakshmi for at the celebration of Divali. Which things do the children think it would be appropriate to ask for?

NOTES ON THE PHOTOCOPIABLE PAGES

Word cards
PAGES 51-53

These cards show the key words that the children will encounter when working on the unit:
- words relating to religious celebrations
- words for the artefacts used in different celebrations.

Read through the word cards with the children to familiarise them with the key words of the unit. Ask which words the children have heard before and clarify any words they do not understand. Encourage the children to add their own word cards to create a 'Celebrations' word bank.

Activities
- Cut out the cards and laminate them. Use them as often as possible when talking about ways in which people can belong to a particular religion, group or organisation.
- Encourage the children to match the word cards to the pictures in the Resource Gallery.
- Use the word cards for displays about 'Celebrations'.

The Nativity story
PAGE 54 

The photocopiable page shows a series of six boxes depicting the events of the nativity story; Mary and Joseph on the journey to Bethlehem; being turned away from an inn; being welcomed by an innkeeper; the angels bringing the good news to the shepherds; three kings seeing a star; the nativity scene with the baby Jesus in a manger. One of the levels of success for Key Stage 1 children is their ability to retell a story. This activity sheet can be used as part of an assessment exercise to test recall skills.

Activities
- Photocopy the sheet onto stiff card. Cut up and ask the children to sequence the pictures.
- Ask the children to retell the story using the cards as prompts. Less able children can choose to describe a single scene from the cards.
- Use the cards to plan a role-play, giving each small group one of the cards to act out.
- Talk about the feelings of the characters at each stage of the story.

Remembering Passover
PAGE 55

There are ten pictures associated with Passover on this photocopiable page. Two of the pictures show the two main characters in the Passover story – the Pharaoh of Egypt and Moses. Of the remaining eight pictures, four link to the story: the slaves making bricks and cement; the slaves sweating and crying at the bitterness of slavery; a woman making flat or unleavened bread ready for the meal; and roasted lamb – the meat that was eaten with the flat bread for the meal before the escape from Egypt. The remaining four pictures show how these experiences of the Hebrew slaves are remembered in the Passover Seder today: the haroset (cement), salt water (sweat and tears), matzot (unleavened bread), and the shankbone (the roasted lamb). Use this sheet in a variety of ways including as an assessment exercise, testing the children's ability to recall both the story about Passover and the items on the Seder table.

Activities
- Photocopy the sheet on to stiff card and cut out the picture boxes. Give each group of children a set of cards and ask them to match up the pairs of pictures.
- Copy the story cards and the Seder cards onto different coloured card to help less able children.

▶ Use these images as a starting point for group role-plays or a mime game. Give each group one of the cards which depicts the story of the Hebrews in Egypt. The group has to enact the scene shown and the rest of the class have to guess the scene. More able children could guess the links with the Seder meal.
▶ Use the cards as prompts to tell the story of Passover.
▶ Give more able children the cards which relate to the Seder meal, and ask them to draw the pictures of the story which explain why these items are on the table.

Design an Id-ul-Fitr card

PAGE 56

Muslim families send Id cards on the festival of Id-ul-Fitr. Using the illustrations and greetings on this sheet, the children can make (or gain inspiration for making) their own Id cards.

Activities

▶ Photocopy and separate the illustrations and the greetings on the worksheets. Discuss with the children the importance of each of the illustrations for Muslims. Ask the children to make an Id card.
▶ Share the resulting Id cards with the rest of the class and ask the children to explain why they have chosen their illustrations.

Following the moon

PAGE 57

The moon is important in Islam. Together with the star, it is part of the symbol for Islam and it is the means by which Muslims mark the start and finish of the months. The moon is particularly important therefore during Ramadan – the months of fasting during daylight hours. Many children have little experience of darkness and moonlight today, as our streets are well lit far into the night. The photocopiable page is designed to encourage the children to become aware of the natural world and in particular the phases of the moon. This increased awareness will provide some insight into the consciousness of Muslims.

Activities

▶ Photocopy and enlarge this activity sheet for display in the classroom.
▶ Discuss with the children the different phases of the moon. Make links between these phases and the times of the moon rising according to the time of year.
▶ Ask the children to notice the phase of the moon during the evening when this unit is taught and plot this on their own copy of the chart. Repeat this over a period of time to note the changes in the moon.

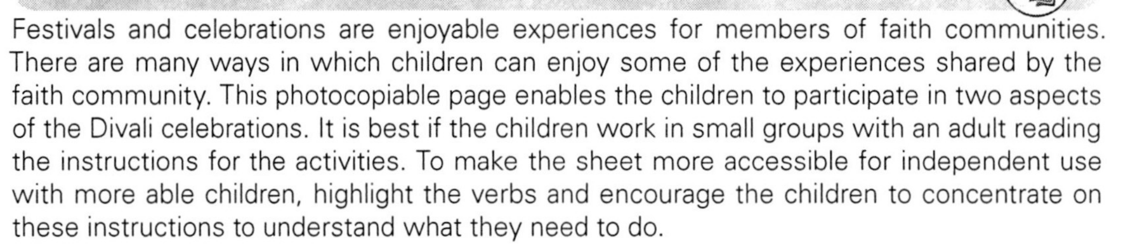

Celebrating Divali

PAGE 58

Festivals and celebrations are enjoyable experiences for members of faith communities. There are many ways in which children can enjoy some of the experiences shared by the faith community. This photocopiable page enables the children to participate in two aspects of the Divali celebrations. It is best if the children work in small groups with an adult reading the instructions for the activities. To make the sheet more accessible for independent use with more able children, highlight the verbs and encourage the children to concentrate on these instructions to understand what they need to do.

Activities

▶ Make some simple sweets for Divali with the children. These sweets are uncooked and can therefore be made by very young children. Be aware of any allergies – if in doubt, omit the food colouring.
▶ Make crêpe flower garlands and encourage the children to present them to other children to promote sharing and giving. Cut the crêpe circles in preparation for this activity as they will be difficult for children to cut out.
▶ Hold a Divali party with a selection of different foods (including any homemade sweets), lights and decorations. Share this with other classes or use these items as a basis for a class assembly to show parents or the rest of the school.

Celebration word cards (1)

Celebration word cards (2)

Celebration word cards (3)

fast
sunrise
sunset
zakat
Divali
puja
diva lamps
Lakshmi

The Nativity story

▶ Cut out these pictures and put them in the correct order.

Remembering Passover

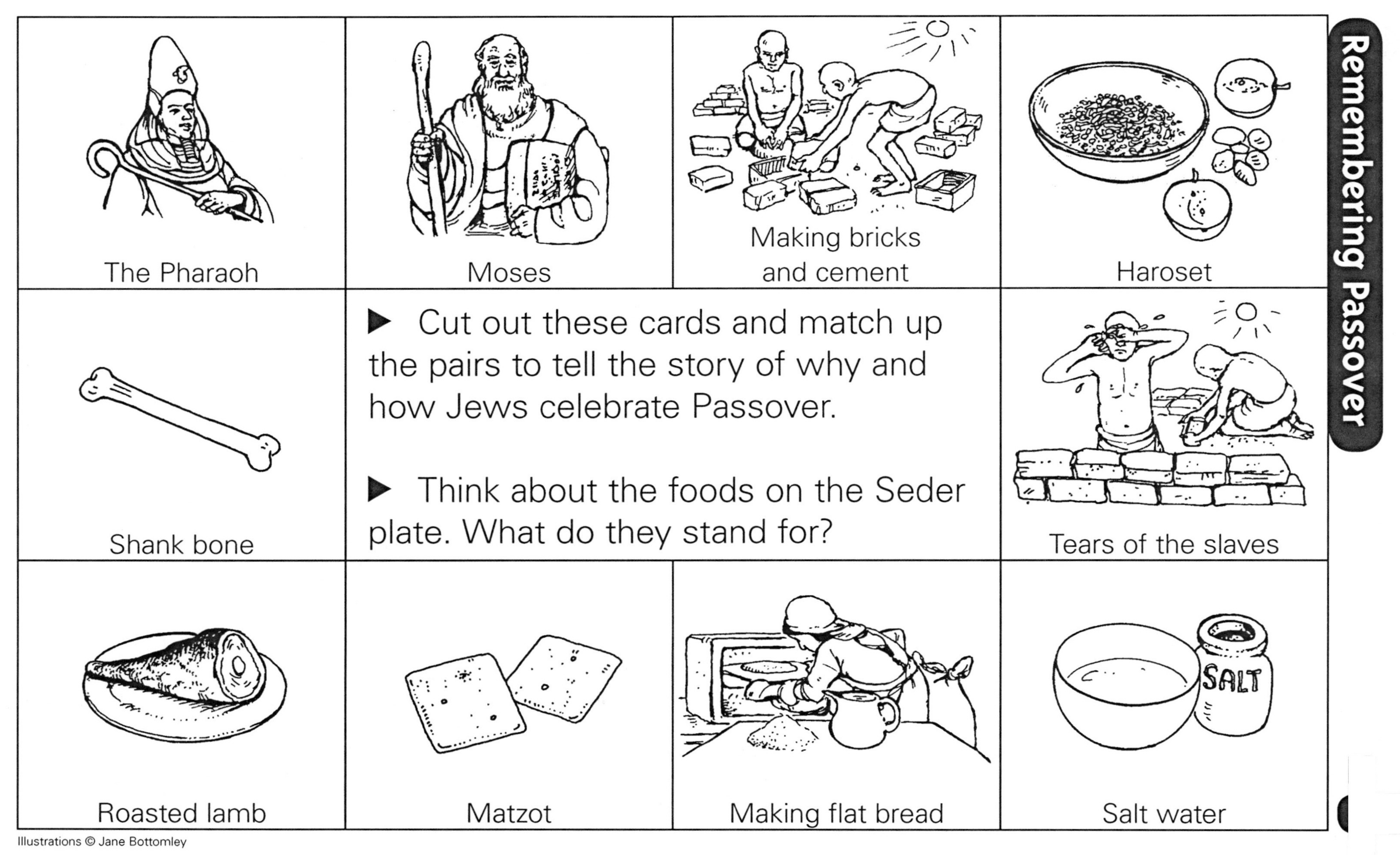

▶ Cut out these cards and match up the pairs to tell the story of why and how Jews celebrate Passover.

▶ Think about the foods on the Seder plate. What do they stand for?

Illustrations © Jane Bottomley

Design an Id-ul-Fitr card

▶ Cut out these greetings and pictures to design your own Id cards.

Following the moon

▶ Use this table to record how the moon changes in the month of ______

Monday	Tuesday	Wednesday	Thursday	Friday	Saturday	Sunday

Cresent moon ☾ Half moon ◗ Full moon ○

Celebrating Divali

Try this easy recipe for Divali sweets

▶ Measure out equal amounts of icing sugar and dessicated coconut. Mix them together.
▶ Add drops of condensed milk as you mix the sugar and coconut until it forms a firm paste.
▶ If you want, you can add some food colouring. Divide your mixture into smaller batches if you want to try different colours.
▶ Roll pieces of the paste into balls. Put your sweets into cake cases and leave to set.
▶ Finally, enjoy your sweets by sharing them with your friends and family!

Make a paper flower garland

▶ Cut out circles of different coloured crêpe paper. Scrunch up the paper to add some texture.
▶ Stick two or three circles together in the middle – not around the edges!
▶ Hold the circles in the centre and tease the edges out to form the petals of your paper flowers.
▶ Thread the 'flowers' along a long piece of string (about 1m). Keep adding paper flowers until you have enough for a garland that can go over your head. Tie the ends of the string together.
▶ Put your garland on your neighbour and greet them with the words, 'Namaste'.

PLACES OF WORSHIP

Content and skills

This chapter continues the theme of belonging by focusing on places of worship in Christianity, Judaism and Islam. The activities address the questions: *What are the special places for Christians, Jews and Muslims? Who are the leaders or key figures within these communities? How do Christians, Jews and Muslims express their beliefs in practice?*

Visits to places of worship are common approaches to teaching and learning in religious education at Key Stage 1. Through such visits the children are able to develop their use of religious words and phrases; identify features of religion; identify how religion is expressed in different ways yet also develop an awareness of the similarities between religions.

This chapter encourages the children to think about what it means to belong to a family and to a faith community. It aims to provide an insight into what it means to worship within Christianity, Judaism and Islam. It therefore relates to the breadth of study in the non-statutory national framework for religious education which states that Christianity and at least one other principal religion should be taught at Key Stage 1. The work supports the framework's themes of belonging, symbol, leaders and teachers, and the framework's experiences and opportunities – especially visiting places of worship and listening and responding to visitors from local faith communities. These are themes and experiences found in most locally agreed syllabuses for religious education, which form the legal requirement for teaching religious education.

The teacher's notes contain background information about the resources and include ways of using them as a whole class, for group work or as individuals. Some of the activities link with other areas of the curriculum, such as literacy and art and design. Wherever possible, the activities encourage the children to ask questions and develop an enquiring approach to their learning.

Resources on the CD-ROM

The resources include exterior and interior features of places of worship from Christianity, Judaism and Islam. There are also photographs of religious leaders such as a rector, rabbi and imam . These resources serve to develop the children's understanding of religion in the place of worship, and what it means to belong to a faith community.

Photocopiable pages

The photocopiable pages in the book are also provided in PDF format on the CD-ROM and can be printed from there. They include:

- word cards containing essential vocabulary for the unit
- an activity sheet that focuses on places of worship in the local area.

NOTES ON THE CD-ROM RESOURCES

A traditional church, A modern church

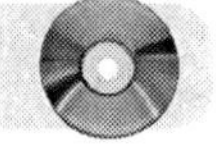

A church is a Christian place of worship. Churches can look different from each other, internally and externally, but most display a cross as a reminder that Christians follow the life and teaching of Jesus Christ. These photographs show an older, traditional (church of England) church that, if seen from above, would be in the shape of a cross, and a modern Methodist church displaying a large cross on its exterior wall.

Discussing the photographs

- Which church do the children think is older/newer? Why do they think so?
- Discuss the differences between the two churches. Look at and compare the shapes of the windows, towers and so on.
- Talk about the cross shapes that are features of both churches. Remind the children of the symbolism of the cross to Christians.

Activities

- Look at a map of your local area and identify the location of the churches.
- Make a list of the names of local churches and identify which churches are named after saints. Find out about these saints together.
- Visit a local church and compare this church to the photographs on the CD. If possible, try to visit two contrasting churches, or a Salvation Army Citadel, to compare different Christian places of worship.
- Using the photographs as guides, and boxes or other reclaimed materials, make two simple models of churches to show the differences in style. The traditional style church will be cross shaped.

Inside a church

The photograph shows the interior of the traditionally-shaped church. Beneath the window at the east end of the church is the sanctuary – the area separated from the congregational area by the wooden altar rail. Inside the sanctuary is the altar; in this photo it is a wooden table, but often it is a stone structure. The altar is the 'table' from which the priest will bless the bread and the wine for holy communion. Behind the altar is a painting of the Last Supper. In front of the altar rail, on the left, is a large stone pulpit from which the sermon is preached. On the right is another stone structure and it might have been from here that the Bible was traditionally read. In front of this is a wooden lectern with the white fabric bookmarkers; the Bible would be placed here and read to the congregation. The area with pews (seats for the congregation) is called the nave, from the Latin word 'navis' meaning 'ship', and the roof in this part of a church often looks like an upturned ship.

Discussion points

- Discuss the different parts of the church in the photograph.
- Talk about the activities that take place in the church, linking them with the areas of the church.
- Discuss any churches that the children have visited, commenting on the similarities and differences between these and the church in this photograph.

Activities

- Learn the words for different parts of the church: the altar, pulpit, lectern, nave.
- Label the picture with the different activities that take place in the church: such as eating bread and drinking wine, reading the Bible, singing, and praying.
- Make a large floor plan of the church with the key places labelled.
- Visit a church and compare it with the key places seen in the photograph.

Stained glass window: Jesus and the children, Stained glass window: Showing charity

Stained glass windows often illustrate sayings and stories from the Bible. The 'Stained glass window: Showing charity' shows two images illustrating the sayings of Jesus: 'I was hungry and you gave me meat; I was thirsty and you gave me drink'. These words are inscribed beneath each window. The four small windows show lilies – a symbol of purity and sometimes a symbol of the Virgin Mary.

The 'Stained glass window: Jesus and the children' shows the story of the women bringing their children to Jesus to be blessed, which is based on verses in the Gospel of Luke (18:15-17). Originally stained glass windows were designed to 'tell stories' to people who were unable to read them for themselves.

Discussing the photographs

- Ask the children to describe what is happening in each of the windows.
- Explain the stories depicted in each window.
- Talk to the children about the symbols in the windows, for example, the lilies – a symbol of purity; and the halos over the heads of Jesus and the disciples.

Activities

- Ask the children to retell the story told by each of the windows.
- Create tableaux of the pictures. Select children to role-play the characters and invite the

rest of the class to show them how to stand to represent the pictures.

- Ask the children to imagine and role-play what each of the characters would say.
- Choose a favourite story from the Bible such as 'The Lost Son' or 'The Good Samaritan' and challenge the children to design their own stained glass window. Read the chosen story and ask the children to decide the most important scene. Discuss what images and colours might be used to show this scene.
- Visit a church to look at and make simple sketches of the stained glass windows.

Priest

This picture shows the Reverend Brian Manning who was rector of St Peter's Church in Cockfield, Suffolk. In some churches the priest may be called a rector, in others, they may be called a vicar. Before a person becomes a priest they have to study for several years. They are then 'ordained' by a bishop before they can begin their work. A priest will lead services in the church on Sundays and on all other days of the week. He, or she, will lead prayers, prepare sermons and conduct baptisms, weddings and funerals. A priest will also care for the people in his or her parish and will visit the sick and the elderly.

Discussing the photograph

- How might the children know that this man is a priest? Do they recognise the symbol of his clerical collar?
- Discuss the different types of duties that the priest has to do within the church and the local community.

Activities

- Plan some questions to ask a local priest about his or her duties and the church services he or she takes.
- Visit a church to meet the priest and provide the children with the opportunity to ask their questions, or invite a priest to the school.
- Make posters entitled, 'A day in the life of a priest'.

A synagogue

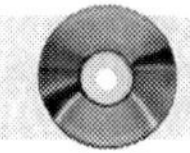

This photograph shows a synagogue, recognisable from the Star of David – the symbol of Judaism, on the roof. Synagogues, like churches, can look very different from each other and it is possible that this synagogue was once a church. Other synagogues may look like a simple hall from outside but there will usually be a Star of David or a menorah (a candlestick with several branches) on the exterior to identify the building as a synagogue.

Discussing the photograph

- Talk about the different types of buildings in the town (such as a Post Office and supermarket) and how people in the community recognise the buildings.
- Discuss with the children the different symbols that identify places of worship. Indicate the Star of David in the photograph, which shows that this building is a synagogue.
- Using the photograph, discuss with the children how, without the Star of David, people might think the building was a church.

Activities

- Ask the children to create a 'special place' through painting, model-making using shoeboxes or by transforming the home corner. Create a sign to show that this is a special place.
- Look on a map of the local area to see whether there is a synagogue. Does the map use a symbol for the synagogue?
- Visit a local synagogue and look for the symbol outside the building that shows that it is a place of worship for Jews.

Inside a synagogue

The photograph shows the interior of a very large synagogue in central London. In the far wall, there is a large cupboard – the Ark. This is the most important part of the synagogue

as the Ark contains the Torah scrolls, the sacred scriptures for the Jews. When they are not being read, the Torah scrolls are dressed in velvet or silk covers and kept in the Ark.

In front of the Ark and facing it is the bimah (reading desk), from which the Torah is read during the service. On the right of the Ark is a stone pulpit (similar to ones found in a church) from which the Rabbi will preach a sermon.

In an Orthodox synagogue, men and women will sit separately. In a Reform synagogue, men and women sit together. This picture shows a Reform synagogue, where the men and women sit together.

Discussing the photograph

- Look at the photograph and talk to the children about the different parts of the synagogue.
- Discuss the different activities that take place in the synagogue – for example, reading from the Torah, preaching a sermon, singing and prayer.
- Make links between these activities and the different parts of the synagogue.

Activities

- Make word cards for the different activities which take place in the synagogue.
- Read a story from the Torah that might be read during the Shabbat (Sabbath) service. The Five Books of Moses that comprise the Torah are also the first five books of the Old Testament in the Christian Bible.
- Visit a local synagogue to look at and compare the different features of the building with those shown in the photograph.

A rabbi

This is a picture of a female rabbi from a Reform synagogue. In Orthodox synagogues, there are no women rabbis. The rabbi is shown wearing her prayer shawl, and the capel she is wearing on her head is just visible. The most important part of the prayer shawl are the 'tzizit' or tassels on the four corners of the shawl, seen clearly in this picture. The knots on the tzizit are reminders of the commandments which every Jew should follow.

The word 'rabbi' means 'teacher' and it is the role of the rabbi to ensure that scripture, the Torah, is read during services and explained to the congregation. A rabbi will lead services, preach sermons, conduct bar or bat mitzvahs when boys of thirteen and girls of twelve 'come of age', conduct weddings and funeral services. Rabbis will also care for their congregation, so they will visit the sick and the elderly.

Discussing the photograph

- Talk together about the special clothes which indicate that the rabbi is a religious leader.
- Talk with the children about the work of the rabbi within the synagogue and within the local Jewish community.

Activities

- Plan a series of questions to ask a rabbi about his or her work.
- Visit a synagogue to meet a rabbi or invite a rabbi to visit the children in school to answer their questions.
- Create a poster entitled, 'A day in the life of a rabbi'.

A mosque

This is a photograph of the Central London Mosque in Regent's Park, London. The mosque has a traditional dome shape and a traditionally-shaped minaret beside it. Not all mosques look the same as this. Some mosques may have been originally built for other purposes, such as a community hall or large terraced houses. Usually there will be Arabic writing or the crescent moon and star, the symbol of Islam, on the exterior to identify the building as a mosque. The crescent moon can just be seen on top of the minaret in the photograph. The minaret is a tall tower from which the muezzin gives the Call to Prayer five times a day. Most mosques will not have a traditionally shaped minaret like this one, and the Call to Prayer will be given inside the mosque or given over a loud speaker to call all Muslims to prayer.

Discussing the photograph

▶ Talk to the children about their own special places and what makes their places special to them. How do they feel when they are in their special place?
▶ Explain that this photograph shows a special place for Muslims where they come to pray. Ask the children to describe the mosque.
▶ Talk with the children about the importance of the minaret and the muezzin who calls the people to prayer five times a day.

Activities

▶ Visit a local mosque and compare the outside features of the building with those that can be seen in the photograph.
▶ Take photographs of the crescent moon and star – symbols which usually feature in a mosque.
▶ Make a frieze of domed shapes and minarets for the classroom.

Clocks showing times of prayer, Prayer times in Arabic

Muslims pray five times a day at specific times of the day: firstly, after dawn but before sunrise; at midday; at mid-afternoon; at sunset; and finally in the evening. By praying five times a day, a Muslim feels the presence of God throughout the day. The clocks remind the Muslims coming to the mosque about the times during which prayers should be made. The midday prayer time on Fridays is when all Muslims try to attend the mosque.

Discussing the photograph

▶ Talk to the children about the pattern of their day, from the time they wake up, to the time they go to bed.
▶ Discuss the occasions during a day when the children or their parents check their watches or clocks as a reminder to do particular things.
▶ Talk to the children about the different clocks in the mosque, which remind Muslims about the times for prayer.
▶ Explain that one photograph shows regular clock faces, and the other shows the times in Arabic.
▶ Invite the children to tell the time on each of the clocks.

Activities

▶ Challenge the children to make a timetable of their day, using clock faces.
▶ Learn the different times of the day when Muslims pray, such as before sunrise, at noon, mid-afternoon.
▶ Make a timetable of the times of day when Muslims pray. If possible, sit quietly at noon to remember all the Muslims in the world who are praying at this time.

Praying in a mosque

The photograph shows Muslims praying in the mosque. The alcove at the far end of the room shows the 'qiblah' (the direction of Makkah and the direction which Muslims should face when praying). The carpet design comprises individual prayer mats and Muslims stand in rows to perform prayer. Prayer consists of a number of body movements: standing, bowing with hands on the knees, prostration (kneeling with one's head touching the ground and then sitting back on one's heels). The positions show the individual's submission to Allah (God). The picture shows men praying. Women pray separately in another room. The clocks indicating the times for prayer are seen on the right of the quiblah. Praying together is one symbol of the 'Ummah' or community in Islam.

Discussing the photograph

▶ Discuss with the children what they can see in the picture, such as the layout of the room, the clocks and the people.
▶ Talk to the children about the position of the men in the picture and why their position suggests that they might be praying.
▶ Make links between the different features of the picture – the clocks, the qiblah and the men praying.

Activities

- Use a compass on a prayer mat, or a regular compass to find the direction of Makkah.
- Make a visual display that shows the different ways in which people of different faiths pray.
- Talk with the children about how it must feel to be praying alongside everyone else in your religious community.

An imam

An imam is a Muslim from within the local community who is respected by the other Muslims for his knowledge of Islam and his practice of the faith. The imam is the person who stands in front of the qiblah, the congregation stands in rows behind him. He leads the communal prayers and all the Muslims follow his actions. An imam will also deliver a sermon, teaching about Allah and how Muslims should lead their lives.

Discussing the photograph

- Talk to the children about what they can see in the picture and whether there are clues as to the religion of the person shown. They might recognise the picture of Makkah on the wall hanging, or the Arabic writing.
- Talk together about the qualities that the children think would make a person a good leader.
- Talk about the imam and the qualities that make him a leader of his community.

Activities

- Talk about the qualities of a good leader. Discuss why these qualities are so important and ask for examples of people who show some of these qualities – whether children in the same class or national figures.
- Ask the children to devise questions to ask an imam about his work in a mosque.
- Visit a local mosque to question the imam or invite an imam to the school.
- Write a short report about 'A day in the life of an imam'.

NOTES ON THE PHOTOCOPIABLE PAGES

Word cards

PAGES 65-66

These cards show key words that the children will encounter when working on the unit:

- words relating to places and leaders of worship
- words relating to prayer.

Read through the word cards with the children to familiarise them with the key words of the unit. Ask which words the children have heard before and clarify any they don't understand.

Activities

- Cut out the cards and laminate them. Use them as often as possible when talking about prayer and different places of worship.
- Encourage the children to match the word cards to the pictures in the Resource Gallery.
- Use the word cards for displays about 'Places of worship'.

Places of worship where I live

This activity raises awareness of places of worship in the local area. Ideally, it should be done with an enlarged map of the local area or else, create a large map with the children.

Activities

- Cut out the boxes and position them on a large map of the local area to learn where local places of worship are situated. Identify the correct faiths to these places of worship.
- Ask the children to use the blank boxes to draw their own symbols to represent a place of worship, or to show a place of worship from a faith different from the ones shown.
- The pictures of the places of worship can be used as a stimulus for further work. For example, surround a picture with word labels that describe that place of worship, or use them as a starting point for a display on 'Places of worship in our local area'.

Worship word cards (1)

SCHOLASTIC
PHOTOCOPIABLE

Worship word cards (2)

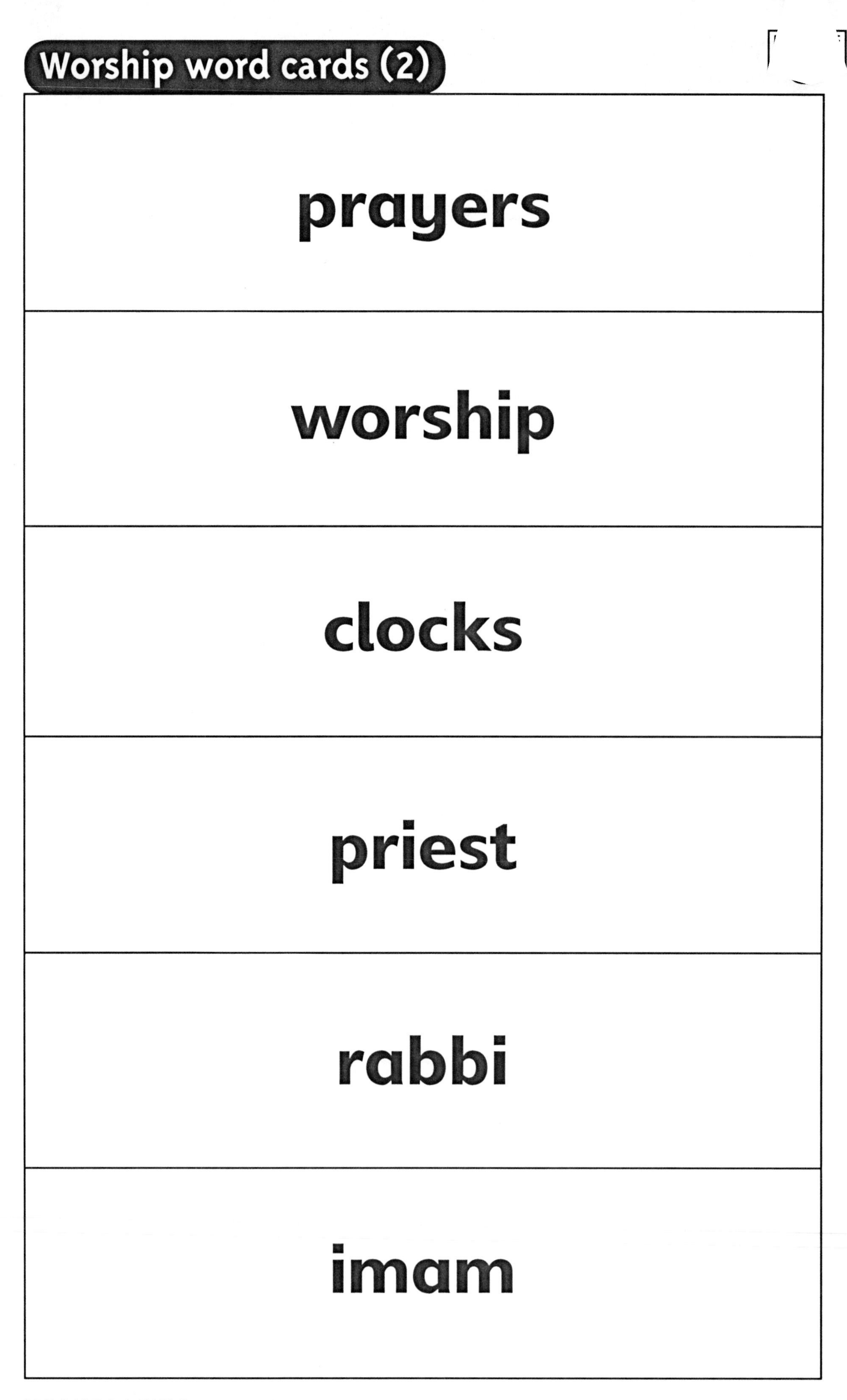

Places of worship where I live

▶ Cut out these places of worship and symbols.

▶ Stick them on a big map of your local area to show where the different places of worship are near your school.

▶ Use the blank boxes to draw other pictures and symbols for places of worship.

SPECIAL BOOKS AND STORIES

Content and skills

This chapter addresses questions about 'authority' in religion – authority in the form of books and stories, which act as guides for faith communities. The discussions and activities in this chapter encourage the children to reflect on questions such as: *What is the Bible and what does it mean to Christians? What is in the Torah scrolls and why are they important to Jews? How was the Qur'an revealed to the Prophet Muhammad, and why is it sacred for Muslims?*

Learning about religion through learning about sacred books and reading special stories is a common approach to religious education at Key Stage 1. The approach enables children to enter imaginatively into religious stories including one example from Hinduism. The children will learn to retell the stories orally, through role-play and through visual images. They can also be helped to consider the importance of the stories and the sacred texts from which they come for members of faith communities.

This chapter encourages the children to think about their own special books and stories and the sacred books and texts of others. Religious stories are profound expressions of religious belief and the basis of religious practice and moral guidance. Learning about and reading from sacred texts therefore can contribute to the children's understanding about local faith communities, their beliefs, religious rituals and moral guidelines.

The chapter enables the children to explore a range of religious stories and sacred writings within Christianity, Judaism and Islam. The chapter relates to the theme of story in the non-statutory national framework for religious education, a theme and approach found in all locally agreed syllabuses for religious education.

The teachers' notes contain background information about the resources and include ways of using them as a whole class, for group work or as individuals. Some of the activities link with other areas of the curriculum, such as literacy and art and design. Wherever possible, the activities encourage the children to ask questions and develop an enquiring approach to their learning.

Resources on the CD-ROM

The resources include photographs of the sacred writings in Christianity, Judaism and Islam, namely the Bible, Torah scroll and the Qur'an.

Photocopiable pages

The photocopiable pages in the book are also provided in PDF format on the CD-ROM and can be printed from there. They include:

- word cards containing essential vocabulary for the unit
- a story about creation
- a story about Joseph and his coat
- a story about Jesus and his disciples
- a story about Moses and the Passover
- a story about Muhammad and the Angel Jibril
- a story about Rama and Sita.

NOTES ON THE CD-ROM RESOURCES

Children's Bibles, A Bible story

The Bible is the holy scripture for Christians. It is in two parts – the Old Testament and The New Testament. The Old Testament contains stories of the Jewish people and Prophets, such as Abraham and Moses; religious laws in the books of Deuteronomy and Leviticus; and poetry such as the Psalms. The New Testament tells about the birth, life, teaching, death and resurrection of Jesus and about the early Christian church.

The Bible is read in churches during services and at home by individual Christians and by families. Some children might be given a bible as a gift at their baptism. The stories in the Bible provide the basis for: Christian festivals such as Christmas and Easter; religious practices such as baptism and the celebration of holy communion; prayers such as The Lord's Prayer and guidelines for life such as the Ten Commandments, the two commandments of Jesus: 'To love God and to love your neighbour as yourself' and in the teachings of the Beatitudes. Christians will understand the Bible in different ways, some seeing it as the literal word of God, while others will understand it as 'inspired' but open to human interpretation.

The picture 'Children's Bibles' shows a collection of Children's Bibles – all colourful with cover pictures that each depict a story from the text. The picture 'A Bible story' shows the story of Jesus fishing with the disciples (based on Luke 5:1-11).

Discussing the pictures

- Talk to the children about their own special books and stories and why they are special to them. The books might have been given by grandparents, or given for a special occasion or perhaps they were the first books that the children could read for themselves.
- Talk to the children about the Bible being a special book for Christians and discuss how the Bible may have different covers for adults and children.
- Discuss the stories represented on the covers of the different Children's Bibles. Talk about the fishing story that is depicted in the picture 'A Bible story'.

Activities

- Make a list of the Bible stories shown on the covers of the Children's Bibles and work out a plan for reading these stories over a period of time.
- Discuss the stories with the children. Ask the children to: identify the most important character(s) in the story; think of questions they would like to ask any of the characters; consider the motivation behind the character/s actions or whether the story is exciting or thought-provoking; think about what might happen next if the story were to continue.
- Role-play one of the stories shown on the covers of the Children's Bibles.
- Visit a church to learn how the Bible is used during the services.

Torah scrolls in the Ark, Unrolled Torah scroll with yad

The photographs show the Torah, the sacred scripture for Jews. The word 'Torah' means 'teaching'. The Torah scrolls are written in Hebrew and contain the five books of Moses: Genesis, Exodus, Leviticus, Numbers and Deuteronomy. For Jews, these books provide teachings about God and guidelines of how to live according to God's commandments. The books can also be found in the Christian Bible, at the start of the Old Testament.

The Torah scrolls have velvet or silk covers, often in blue or red. The covers are decorated with Hebrew writing and often two tablets, which are a reminder of the commandments which Moses brought down from Mount Sinai, written on tablets of stone. Silver bells are often attached to the wooden tops of the scrolls and a silver breastplate over the scrolls when the Torah is not being read. Both can be seen in 'Torah scrolls in the Ark'. The Ark, a large wooden cupboard in the synagogue, usually faces towards Jerusalem. When Jews pray in the synagogue, they face towards the Ark and Torah scrolls.

The scrolls are made from parchment and are handwritten, so must be handled with great care. The reader will therefore use a pointer or 'yad' to point to the words. 'Yad' means 'hand' in Hebrew. The words in the Torah are the words of God. If they become smudged, the scroll is no longer fit for religious use or 'kosher', and cannot be used until repaired. When the scroll is fully opened, it is almost the length of a football pitch.

Discussing the photographs

▶ Talk to the children about their favourite or special books and stories and how they treat something which is special to them.
▶ Discuss with the children how the special book for Jews is in the form of a scroll.
▶ Introduce the children to the Ark as a place in the synagogue where the scrolls are kept when they are not being read.
▶ Discuss with the children the importance of protecting the handwritten script by using a 'yad' or pointer.

Activities

▶ Visit a local synagogue to look at the Ark.
▶ Ask a rabbi or representative in the synagogue to show the Torah scrolls and the Hebrew writing on the scrolls.
▶ Ask a Jewish parent or representative to read some Hebrew to the children.
▶ Practise writing some letters from the Hebrew alphabet.
▶ If a visit is not possible, watch a video showing the scrolls being taken from the Ark. A useful video is *Watch! Places for Worship* (BBC Educational).
▶ Read or listen to some stories from the Torah, told to Jewish children. For example, the story of Abraham, or Moses, or the story of Joseph and his brothers.

Qur'an on a stand, An open Qur'an

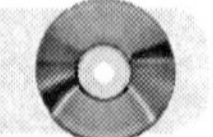

For Muslims, the Qur'an, written in Arabic, contains the word of Allah, as revealed to the Prophet Muhammad. It is regarded as Allah's final revelation to humans, and thus treated with the utmost respect. It is the duty of every Muslim to read the Qur'an and to understand its teaching. The Qur'an is a guide for Muslims as to how they should live their lives, how and when they should pray, how they should fast and give zakat to the poor. It includes stories and references to the Prophets such as Ibrahim (Abraham) and Nuh (Noah), prophets shared by Jews and Christians too – although some of the stories may have slight differences in the Muslim tradition.

The Qur'an is arranged in 114 chapters or 'surahs'. To read the Qur'an is a form of worship and many Muslims learn to recite the Qur'an by heart. Muslim children attend a religious school in the evenings to learn to recite the Qur'an. The Qur'an is often placed on a stand while it is read, as seen in 'Qur'an on a stand'. When not being used, the Qur'an is usually wrapped in cloth and placed on a high shelf, above shoulder height, as a mark of respect for its importance.

Discussing the photographs

▶ Discuss where and how the children keep their most treasured books or objects.
▶ Look at the pictures and explain that the Qur'an is a special book in the Islamic faith.
▶ Talk to the children about how Muslims keep the Qur'an on a high shelf and perform 'wudu', a washing ritual before reading it.
▶ Introduce the idea that Muslims believe that the Qur'an is the actual word of Allah, revealed to the Prophet Muhammad.

Activities

▶ Visit a local mosque and ask the imam or a member of the community to recite an extract in Arabic.
▶ Listen to or read a story from the Qur'an. It is best to use a retelling of a story specifically for children such as that on photocopiable page 79 'Muhammad is visited by Angel Jibril'.
▶ Invite a Muslim to retell their favourite story from the Qur'an. Ask them to explain why the Qur'an is important to him or her.

NOTES ON THE PHOTOCOPIABLE PAGES

Story word cards

PAGES 73-74

These cards show key words that the children will encounter when working on the unit:
- words relating to special religious books
- names of key characters in the special stories in this section.

Read through the word cards with the children to familiarise them with the key words of the unit. Ask the children for words they do not understand.

Activities

- Cut out the cards and laminate them. Use them as often as possible when reading stories from the Bible, Torah or Qur'an.
- Encourage the children to match the word cards to the pictures in the Resource Gallery.
- Use the word cards for displays about 'Special books and stories'.

Story of Creation

PAGE 75

The story of Creation is told in the book of Genesis and is told by both Jews and Christians. The story tells about God creating the world and this is central to Jewish and Christian belief. God is a Creator and it is as a result of his command that all things were made. The belief that God created the natural world and then the first people, Adam and Eve, has implications for Jews and Christians on how they should live their lives. The belief that human beings were created in the image of God means that humans have a responsibility to care, not only for the natural world but also for other humans and for animals.

Activities

- Before reading the story, ask the children to identify an aspect of nature special to them – animals, sunshine, trees, rain.
- Ask the children to draw a picture of an aspect of nature that is special to them and to write a sentence explaining why it is special. If applicable, ask them how they could care for this aspect of nature.
- Make a collage of pictures, paintings and poems about the natural world.

Jesus and his friends

PAGE 76

This story is about Jesus choosing his disciples (based on the Gospel of Luke 5:1-11). Jesus meets the fishermen Simon, Andrew, James and John as they are washing their nets. He asks them to take him out in their boat so that the crowd can see and hear him preaching. Then Jesus tells them to put out their fishing nets. Despite earlier failure, the men catch a large number of fish. Jesus tells them that they will now be catching men. This is the beginning of Jesus' teaching and healing ministry and suggests that Jesus chose simple, hardworking men to support him in his work.

Activities

- Before reading the story, ask the children to identify the qualities that they look for in friends.
- Discuss the reasons why Jesus might have chosen Simon, Andrew, James and John to be his disciples or special friends. In the story, what qualities do the fishermen show?
- Ask the children to think of some questions that they would like to ask the fishermen.

Moses leads the slaves to freedom

PAGE 77

The story tells of the time when the Jews were slaves in Egypt working for the Pharaoh. God sends Moses to the Pharaoh to ask for the slaves' freedom, but when the Pharaoh refuses, God sends plagues to the land. The final plague kills the firstborn animal and person in every Egyptian home and the Egyptians are so distressed that the slaves are able to escape from Egypt. For Jews, this is the time when God, through Moses, intervened in history to free the Jewish people – an event which is commemorated each year at the festival of Passover. The story is told in the book of Exodus.

Activities

- Look at the picture of the Seder plate (provided on the CD), and discuss the symbolic food items on the plate. Make links between the items on the plate and the story of Moses.
- Discuss the characters of Moses and the Pharaoh.
- Role-play part of the story, for example, the first time Moses approaches the Pharaoh.

Joseph and his brothers

PAGE 78

The story of Joseph is found in the Old Testament, Genesis 37. It tells about family jealousy of a younger favoured brother who, in turn, dreams of his own greatness and superiority over his brothers. The brothers throw Joseph into a pit and then sell him to merchants who carry him down to Egypt. The story on the photocopiable page ends here.

Tell the rest of the story to the children – how Joseph works in Egypt and through his skill at interpreting dreams, Joseph encourages the Pharaoh to store corn during the years of plenty – so saving Egypt from disaster when famine strikes. This is a powerful story with strong emotions for the children to discuss and empathise with.

Activities

- Before reading the story, ask the children to talk about their relationships with their brothers and sisters (if they have them).
- Discuss the characters in the story – was Joseph right to tell his brothers his dreams? Were his brothers right to be jealous?
- Listen to the music of *Joseph and his Amazing Technicolour Dreamcoat* composed by Andrew Lloyd Webber (Polydor) and learn some of the songs.

Muhammad is visited by Angel Jibril

PAGE 79

Muslims believe that Allah revealed the Qur'an to the Prophet Muhammad through the Angel Jibril. This is the story of the revelation; it is central to Muslim belief that the Qur'an is the actual revelation of Allah. Angel Jibril visited Muhammad while he was praying, alone in a cave on Mount Hira. Muhammad was initially afraid, but his wife helped him to understand that he was to be a prophet of Allah. Although this is the story of one visit by the Angel, this was one of many revelations.

Activities

- Introduce the context of the story – Makkah was a very busy town and Muhammad liked to go into the mountains to be quiet and to pray.
- Discuss the changing feelings of the Prophet Muhammad throughout the story.
- Make links between the story and the holy book for Muslims, the Qur'an.
- Talk with the children about the times and places when they like to be quiet and where they go to do this.

Rama and Sita

PAGE 80

This story from the Ramayana (a Sanskrit epic) is told at the festival of Divali. It is a story about light conquering darkness, a story about good and evil. The story is about how Ravana, the demon with ten heads, seizes Sita and takes her to his kingdom. Hanuman, the Monkey General, helps Rama to form an army to fight Ravana and to bring Sita home. Small clay lamps, divas, are lit to welcome the couple home – they are symbols of light conquering darkness, good conquering evil. This is also a tale of courage, of Hanuman's smaller and seemingly less powerful army winning the battle over the demon Ravana.

Activities

- Display the pictures 'Diva lamps' and 'Celebrating Divali' (provided on the CD) and read the story of Rama and Sita from photocopiable page 80.
- Role-play the story – use slow motion and non-contact techniques for the fight scenes.
- Retell the story using finger or stick puppets. Create a puppet show for other classes.
- Discuss the qualities of some of the characters such as Lakshmana and Hanuman.

Story word cards (1)

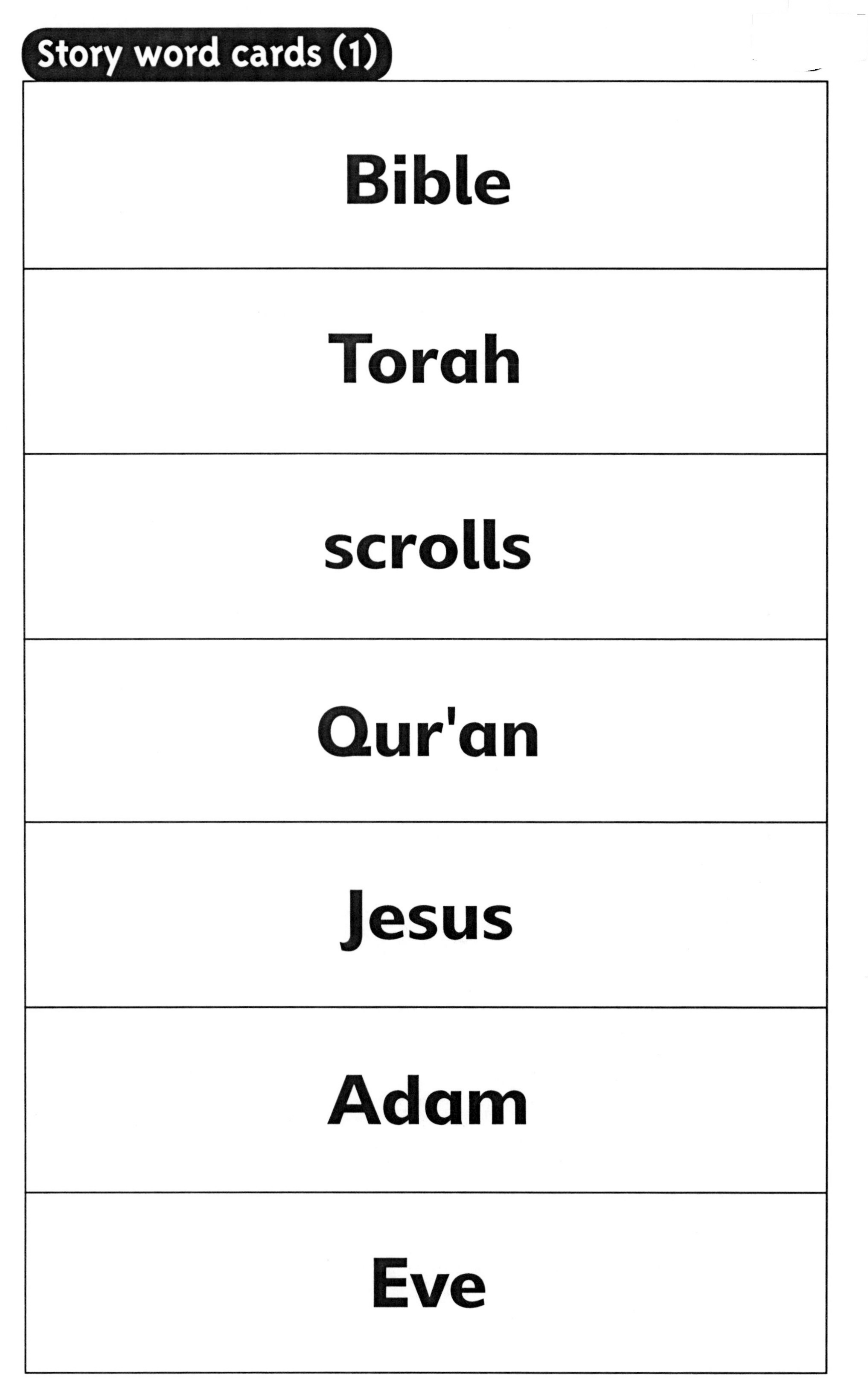

Bible
Torah
scrolls
Qur'an
Jesus
Adam
Eve

Story word cards (2)

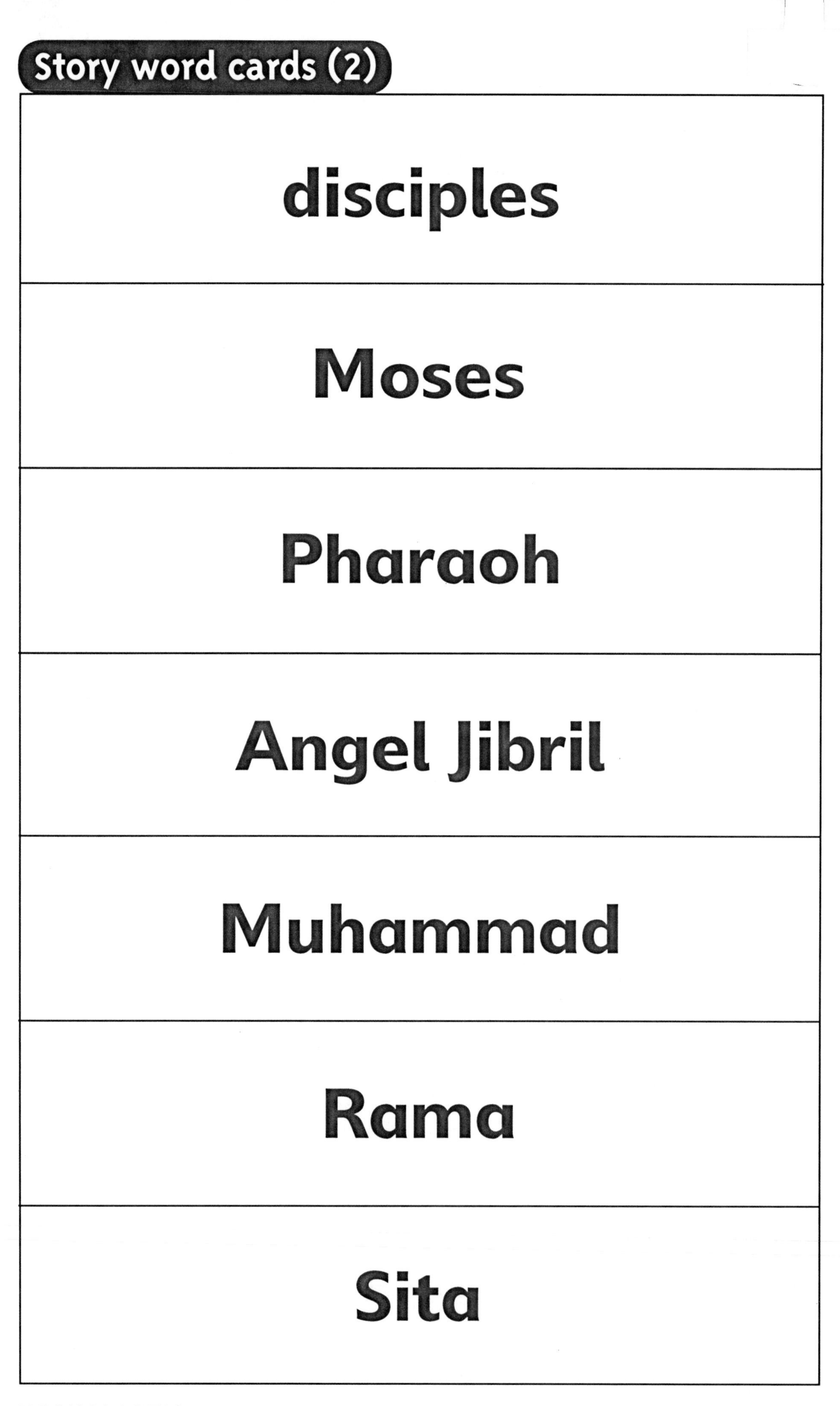

disciples
Moses
Pharaoh
Angel Jibril
Muhammad
Rama
Sita

Story of Creation

This is a story about how God created the world. In the beginning there was nothing. No light, no people, no animals. Everything was in darkness.

God said, 'Let there be light!' And light came. God divided the light from the darkness. He called the light 'Day' and the darkness 'Night'. This was Day One.

God created the waters. They flowed everywhere – there were great seas and swirling streams. Over the waters, God created the sky. And this was Day Two.

The next day, on Day Three, God created the land and looked at it. It needed some grass, trees, plants and flowers. So that is what God created – trees and plants, and flowers in reds, blues, purples and yellows. They all looked wonderful!

On Day Four, God decided to create lights in the sky to make day and night. He threw a big ball of light into the day sky. It made the day bright and sunny. Into the night sky God threw a smaller light, a silver moon, and stars to twinkle in the darkness.

On Day Five, God made fish to swim in the sea – big sharks, small crabs and tiny tiddlers. Then he made birds to fly in the air – great eagles, white doves, blackbirds and little red robins. God blessed them all.

Next, God created all the animals – lions, bears, elephants, cows, monkeys, snakes, and baby rabbits too! God looked at them all and he thought that he needed someone to look after the world he had made. So he created people – a man and a woman. He called the man Adam and the woman Eve. He told them to care for the world, the plants, trees and flowers, the fish and the birds and all the animals. This was an important job for Adam and Eve. This all happened on Day Six.

On Day Seven, God looked at his world. He was pleased! He decided to make the seventh day special – a day of rest, when everyone could remember how God created the world!

Illustration © Jane Bottomley

Jesus and his friends

It was a sunny morning and Jesus was by the Sea of Galilee teaching people about God. There was a large crowd and everyone was pushing to get closer to Jesus.

Jesus saw two boats by the shore and the fishermen were nearby washing their nets. Jesus spoke to one of the men. 'Simon, will you row me out a little way so that everyone can see and hear me?' Simon rowed Jesus out on to the lake and Jesus stood up in the boat so that everyone could see and hear him.

When he had finished speaking to the people, Jesus said to Simon, 'Row the boat out further into deeper water and let the nets out for a catch of fish.'

'It will do no good,' said Simon. 'We fished all night and caught nothing.' But he listened to Jesus and rowed the boat out further into deep water and let the nets out.

Soon the nets were so full of fish that they were almost breaking! Simon had to call other fishermen, his friends James and John, to come and help. There were so many fish that the boats began to sink.

Had Jesus known about the fish?

Simon, James and John were amazed that they had caught so many fish. They knew that Jesus must be a very special person. 'Do not be afraid,' said Jesus. 'Today you have been gathering fish but from now on you will be gathering people.'

Simon, and his brother Andrew, and his friends James and John, all left their boats and followed Jesus. From that day, they would be his special friends, his disciples. They would help him with his work teaching people about God.

Moses leads the slaves to freedom

Many years ago, the Jews were slaves in Egypt. The Pharaoh, king of Egypt, made the slaves work hard in the hot sun. They had to make bricks from mud and straw, and build the pyramids.

God told Moses to ask the Pharaoh to set the Jews free. Moses went to the Pharaoh. He said, 'Let my people go!' But the Pharaoh wanted to keep his slaves, so he said 'No!'

God was angry. He sent plagues to the land of Egypt. First the River Nile turned red like blood and no one could drink the water. Then a plague of frogs jumped into the beds and the cooking pots of the Egyptians. The frogs were followed by swarms of mosquitos which bit everyone, and the mosquitos were followed by swarms of flies which flew everywhere! The cattle of the Egyptians died, and the people and the animals got painful boils. Then came huge hailstones, and locusts which ate all the green plants. And then came darkness which lasted for three whole days!

Each time there was a plague, the Pharaoh was scared. He said that the slaves could go free. But when each plague stopped, he changed his mind again.

God told Moses that there would be one more plague and this would be the worst plague of all. After this plague, the Jews would leave Egypt. They would be free!

Moses told the Jews to prepare for a long journey. Every family made a special meal of lamb cooked with herbs and flat bread – they were in such a hurry that there was not time to let the bread rise!

That night something terrible happened. In every Egyptian family, the firstborn child and the firstborn of every animal died. The Egyptians were shocked and upset. They could do nothing!

The Jews had their chance to escape. While the Egyptians cried over their dead animals and children, Moses led the slaves out of Egypt. They travelled on a very long journey, across rivers and deserts until they reached a new land, the land of Israel. Here they built new cities and new homes. The Jews were no longer slaves – they were free!

Joseph and his brothers

A long time ago, there was a man called Jacob. Jacob had twelve sons and his favourite son was Joseph. His father gave Joseph a beautiful coat. It was brightly coloured and it had long sleeves – long sleeves meant that Joseph did not have to do much work! His brothers were jealous of Joseph!

Joseph was a dreamer – he had lots of dreams, and he always remembered them. One night, Joseph dreamed that he and his brothers were cutting down the corn at harvest time and tying the corn into bundles. In the dream, his brothers' bundles stood in a circle and bowed down to Joseph's bundle in the centre! Did this mean that Joseph was special? His brothers were angry when Joseph told them about this.

Then Joseph had another dream. He dreamed that the Sun, the Moon and eleven stars were bowing down to him. Even his father Jacob was cross this time. 'Does this mean that I and your mother and your brothers will be bowing down to you?' he asked.

Joseph's brothers were angry. They wanted to teach Joseph a lesson. One day, when they were in the fields looking after the sheep, Joseph went to see them. They got hold of him, took off his brightly coloured coat and threw him into a deep pit. Joseph was so scared! Just then, some traders on camels came along and his brothers decided to sell Joseph to them, as a slave.

The brothers did not know what to tell Jacob about his favourite son, so they took Joseph's coat and smeared it with goat's blood. When they arrived home, they gave the coat to Jacob and said they had found it. Jacob thought his son was dead and he wept.

What happened to Joseph? Did he become important?

Well, the traders took him down to Egypt where he worked for the Pharaoh, the king of Egypt. But that's another story...

Muhammad is visited by the Angel Jibril

A long time ago, a man named Muhammad, lived with his wife in the city of Makkah. Makkah was a very busy and noisy city. Sometimes Muhammad liked to get away from the crowded city and go into the mountains. There was a special cave on Mount Hira where Muhammad could be alone to think and pray.

One night, Muhammad was in the cave. He wrapped his cloak around him and fell asleep. Suddenly, a messenger came to Muhammad. It was the Angel Jibril, Allah's messenger. Jibril had an important message for Muhammad.

'Recite,' ordered Angel Jibril.

'I cannot recite,' said Muhammad.

'Recite,' said the angel a second time.

'I cannot recite,' replied Muhammad.

'Recite,' said the angel a third time, holding Muhammad very tightly.

This time, Muhammad began to recite the words taught to him by the angel. Muhammad knew that these words were a message from Allah. He felt as if the words were written on his heart.

When Muhammad left the cave, he was shocked and confused by the angel's visit. He ran down the mountain and told his wife what had happened. She helped Muhammad to understand that he had been chosen by Allah to be a prophet or special messenger.

Muhammad went to the cave many times after that and was visited by the Angel Jibril. The words that Jibril taught Muhammad were written down, at first on stones, leaves and bits of bone and leather. Later, they were written on paper to make a special book called the Qur'an. This book became very precious to Muslims because it contains the very words written down by Muhammad, the words of Allah.

Rama and Sita

Rama and his wife Sita lived in the forest with Rama's brother, Lakshman. One day, Sita saw a beautiful deer. 'Look, Rama, a deer,' she cried. 'Please catch it for me!' Rama ran off into the forest.

Some time later, Sita and Lakshman heard someone calling. It sounded like Rama's voice asking for help. Lakshman took his bow and drew a circle around their hut. 'Stay inside this circle,' he told Sita. 'You will be safe here'.

Sita was left alone. Soon, Ravana, the demon with ten heads, came to Sita's hut. He was dressed in orange robes, like a holy man, so Sita did not recognise him. 'Please give me some food,' he begged. Sita brought a bowl of food to Ravana. As she came close to him, Ravana pulled Sita outside the circle! He carried her off in his flying chariot to his kingdom in Lanka.

When Rama and Lakshman returned to the hut, they could not find Sita anywhere. Hanuman, the Monkey-God, said he would help them. Hanuman followed the trail of Sita's bangles which she had thrown out of the chariot. He found Sita in Lanka, but Ravana would not set her free.

Hanuman asked all the animals in the forest to join an army to fight Ravana. They all agreed to help. Rama, Lakshman, Hanuman and the army of animals travelled to Lanka. When Ravana and his mighty army saw the army of animals, they laughed! 'Look at Rama and his army!' they cried.

There were many battles. At the end of a long fight, Rama put a special arrow in his bow. He shot the arrow at Ravana and Ravana fell down dead! Everyone cheered, 'Rama has killed the demon Ravana!'

Rama found Sita and brought her home again. Everyone was so happy that they lit small diva lamps to show Rama and Sita the way.

'Welcome home, Rama and Sita', they cried.